# Profit Magic

A fable about profits and
the people who create them

Randy Brooks

.

# DEDICATION

Tom Donnelly, Jim Roberts, Lisa Spaulding, Phillip Thrash, Kristi Woodworth and Lynn Noble were among my first employees and all of them joined Directions Research long before it was obvious it would become a great place to work. Joe Sturniolo, Gary Kurlancheek, Vivian Calloway and Jim Nyce all awarded important projects to Directions Research before we really had the proven ability to complete them. The debt I owe to these friends cannot be repaid.

# CONTENTS

# ACKNOWLEDGEMENTS

My wife, Niki Pappas, encouraged me to write this book and waded through the  tortured prose of my first efforts offering only encouragement. The book was edited by Denise Wilde, Carol Poglitsh and Kristi Woodworth who thankfully can spell and punctuate (the author has neither skill). Steve Wilde, Terry McCarthy, and Dr. Eileen Weisenbach Keller read the book at various stages and offered constructive advice. Harry Malt (Harrymaltdrawspictures.Blogspot.com) drew all of the clever illustrations.

.

# PROLOGUE

Peter Profit woke up with a throbbing headache the morning after his first night in Las Vegas. He had all the classic symptoms of a night out on the town – dry mouth, aching head and uneasy stomach – but he was as excited as a kid. For the very first time, Peter had been invited to attend the Las Vegas Profit Convention.

Profits are to businesses as touchdowns are to football teams – the result of the entire team doing everything right. Profits are MAGIC. Profits capture, in one metric, all you need to know about a business. It turns out Profits are *alive*.

From time to time all the Profits from all the largest firms in America get together to compare notes and have a good time. Peter Profit was the living, breathing, money-come-to-life profits created by Owen Enterprises. Owen Enterprises had grown steadily for years, and Peter Profit kept getting bigger and bigger. Finally he was large enough to be invited to the biggest and most important Profit conference in the world!

When Peter walked in to register for the conference, Apple Profit was standing right in front of him. Every small start-up firm in the world was inspired by his story. A couple of kids in a garage founded a firm and years later they were worth more than Microsoft, GE, or IBM. The firm and their Profit were ever so cool. Apple Profit wore jeans and a turtleneck and sported a three-day growth of facial hair that would do Russell Crowe proud. Plus, Apple Profit immediately said hello to Peter and welcomed him!

"Hi, I'm Apple – this is your first time?"

Stunned, Peter replied, "Yes, Mr. Apple, Sir – jeez you're like my hero – uh, uh ..."

"Congratulations on your success and I hope you enjoy the conference. We have a reception in my suite later. Here, take this invitation and join us for a drink."

Apple was then hailed by reporters and dragged away. Peter thought he was going to wet his pants. "Apple spoke to me! Wow! And invited me to a party???!!! This is great!"

The rest of the day passed in a blur of cocktails, music, food, and introductions. Peter met many other Profits and collected so many business cards he lost track. The biggest Profits were the most welcoming. They all praised Peter and wanted to know more about Owen Enterprises, and how it had succeeded in growing Peter to a level which earned him an invitation to the conference.

Maybe their attitudes were best summed up when Hewlett Packard Profit called him over to her table later that night and insisted on buying him a nightcap.

"Congratulations on your success. I read a little about Owen Enterprises in the conference packet and loved the story. I was hoping to get a chance to get to know you a little better," she explained.

"Really? I am so flattered – I mean, jeez, all the big players here have been so nice and I didn't know what to expect and wow ... I ... I mean uh ..."

"Relax, Peter, we all remember how hard it was to start and how exciting it was in the beginning. Well, not all of us. Profits like Coca-Cola, GE and some of the oldest firms can't remember their founding days. But for many of us, watching Profits like you is sort of like getting a new puppy or playing with our grandchildren. The very best years for Profits are often the early ones when the risks seem so real and terrifying. Success or failure hangs in the balance. You see, when firms get really big, they sometimes forget the magic of the creation of Profits in the first place. Then we get to meet you and all the other newcomers and it reminds us of our beginnings. So, can you tell me your story?"

Peter beamed, gulped, and, suddenly for the first time in his life, felt like a grown up (even though she had just called him a puppy)!

"I'll try," Peter said.

# 1 GETTING SOME EXPERIENCE

After leaving college, Owen, future founder of Owen Enterprises, worked for 15 years for Billie Enterprises, a large and respected firm that provided consulting and analytical services to the largest businesses in America. When Owen joined the firm they were growing steadily. Because revenue was strong and because management restrained the growth in overhead, Billie Enterprises was growing. Profits were up every year. Billie Profit was so fit she even ran a marathon! Billie Profit was the acknowledged superstar – the Michael Jordan of the firm.

It was terrific fun in those years. Every year revenues grew, and every year talented new, young and cute staff (Owen was single in those days) joined the firm. Bright, eager and ambitious staff were given outsized opportunities to prove themselves. They had a saying at Billie Enterprises that Owen loved – "throw them in the deep end."

Owen was even sent to work in London after just two years with the firm. He learned to drink wine and met real Italians! They seemed like regular people except they lived in Italy, spoke mainly Italian, and were actual card-carrying Communists! Talk about cool – it was breathtaking. Owen had the time of his life.

When he came back from London he moved steadily up at Billie Enterprises. He spent several years in Chicago, then was selected to open a new office for the firm in Atlanta, and finally was promoted to Executive Vice President with national responsibilities for a small division of the firm. It seemed as if the good times would stretch endlessly into the future.

But gradually something did change at Billie Enterprises. Forty years of regular growth in revenue slowed, stopped, and then revenue began to decline. The CMO (Chief Marketing Officer who was responsible for revenue) began to look old and tired. He took to using a cane! He got moody, too, and claimed it wasn't his fault. Neither the CMO nor the COO (Chief Operating Officer) would take responsibility for what was going on. It was subtle at first, but then it got worse and worse and worse.

One day, a couple of the "best and the brightest" senior people at Billie Enterprises quit to start their own firm. The COO immediately put out the word that "the TRAITORS had never carried their weight and were complaining whiners. We're better off without them." (This is the direct quote from the memo!) This seemed really confusing to Owen who liked and respected the TRAITORS. How could they go from being great members of the team to hated TRAITORS in one day?

Department managers began to quarrel about "whose work that was." Turf battles broke out all over the place. Everyone claimed to be "really, really, really busy." This seemed odd since there was less work to do every year. The "Chiefs" looked bad, but Billie Profit looked worse. Billie Profit began to look very bad, pooped and barely able to walk up a flight of stairs.

The owner of Billie Enterprises was unhappy. What owner could be happy watching Profits shrink every year?

Owen was sick with worry. The once generous bonus plan disintegrated because the owner was not going to "share the wealth" if there was no wealth to share. Morale collapsed and it was no longer fun to go to work.

Owen ran around the company, in effect yelling "Fire, Fire!" and tried to point out things that made no sense to him. Owen had an MBA after all (okay, it was from a state college and not a distinguished, exclusive Ivy League institution, but he had gotten really good grades!) and sometimes he acted like he knew more than the CMO or COO, and this pissed them off. (Sorry for the bad language, but it's true.) The COO decided Owen was a problem, maybe the problem. Nasty meetings took place. Owen became more and more unhappy, and then the worst thing that can happen to a business occurred.

Billie Profit was hospitalized. She was in critical condition. In fact, Billie Profit disappeared. The doctors said she wasn't dead; she had just turned into something called "Losses." There was an ugly red glow in the spot on the bed where Billie had last been seen.

The doctor said, "We just need to catch a break. Sometimes "Losses" simply disappear. Good old Billie Profit might show up, sit up, walk, and maybe even run again."

It was kind of like Lazarus, I guess, but no one alive now had actually seen Lazarus get up and walk, and there was no real proof he couldn't walk in the first place. So a lot of people just worried even more.

The CMO and COO could not bear the pain of firing employees, layoffs, or forcing early retirements. They kept waiting for a break (sort of like hoping for a turnover in a big game when your team is losing). They hoped a big new assignment from a client would appear. Senior management began reading their horoscopes and even consulted with a fortune teller, to see if Billie Enterprises' luck would change. The situation at Billie Enterprises continued to get worse.

Owen didn't think the firm should embrace a formal business plan based on wishing, hoping and luck. Luck, he had heard, was the intersection of Preparation and Opportunity. Wishing for luck did not seem anything like preparation. Opportunities didn't seem to be anywhere on the horizon and, as far as he could see, management was not doing anything to uncover opportunities. They were just sitting in their offices writing nasty, scary memos.

One day, Owen resigned. He was terrified, but he was determined to see if he could do his own thing. Many people thought Owen had lost his mind, but he had some ideas and some ways of doing things others simply would not consider. Owen was going to start his own business!

## 2 CAPITAL

Along with the terror, Owen also felt exhilaration. The last five years at Billie Enterprises had been a nightmare, but he had always had a paycheck. Now he didn't. He was really scared. But his mind was on fire.

He knew the key to starting a business was Capital (a fancy word for money). He knew he had to live and feed his family, and he also had to have some money for the company he was going to start.

It was about this time that he met the Demons – the embodiment of the self doubts that show up and terrify risk takers. His Demons loved preying on him at low moments. Their opening night performance set the tone for a 25-year relationship.

4

"Yeah, right," his Demons said, "You're going to start a company. That's nuts! Get a job! Earn a paycheck. Become a Team Player. You could lose everything!"

Interestingly enough, the Demons only visited in the middle of sleepless nights, when he couldn't do anything. And so he worried. He tried to remember to repeat the famous Will Rogers quote about worry: "Worry is like making payments on a debt that may never come due."

Because step one was Capital (it's always about the money, always) and because he had to live and feed his family, he did a really thorough job of counting his money and investments. He counted everything – even his 401(k) and the equity in his home. Next, he looked at the past two years of spending to see if he could figure out what he was spending and then created a family budget. Finally, he computed the income he had to have every month to make sure his family could stay in their home and pay the bills.

Sadly, he realized there was no money for the expensive French wines he had learned to love in London. Merlot does suck, but it was about $8.00 a bottle. He did some math and found he could have one bottle of French Burgundy a month or 10 bottles of cheap California Merlot. "This running a company is easy!" he thought.

Owen visited with several bankers and one of them made the first of many stunning suggestions outside advisors were to make over the years (but sadly the last such suggestion from a banker).

The Banker asked, "How long do you think it will take you to prove to yourself that you can succeed at this before you throw in the towel?"

Owen was terrified thinking about this, but he had talked to five or six colleagues who had started firms in the last few years including, importantly, the TRAITORS who were now spending winters in St. Barts. They thought 18 months was it. "Succeed in 18 months or give it up. Get a Job. Join the Team."

The Banker then said the stunning thing mentioned earlier: "You said earlier that all of your living expenses would be $4,500 per month. I think that is a little low. Let's make it $5,000 a month. Buy eighteen $5,000 CD's. Have them mature in one month, two months, three months and so forth. Tell your wife this money will be deposited into her checking account each month. It's your, um, paycheck," chuckled the Banker. (Bankers are sick actually.) "Put the rest of your "moola" in the company. That's your capital for Owen Enterprises."

Really, Bankers look rational enough all suited up, but they are just like the junkies on the corner looking for their next fix. All the junkie wants is the drug and all the banker cares about is the money and something called "collateral," which you never have when you actually need it.

Owen was stunned. This was really going to happen. He was going to do this! He was now a

# CAPITALIST

# 3 DEFINITIONS ARE IMPORTANT

Now that he was a business owner and a capitalist, Owen thought he should do some research on what that really was. How was it different from being a man or an employee or a sports fan or a golfer or a Dad?

It turns out a capitalist is one who invests Capital into a business with the expectation of getting a return. The return was divided into two very important piles:

- Profit – Owen could already envision me (a cute baby all warm and cuddly) long before he actually saw me in the flesh.
- Appreciation – presumably if Owen succeeded, the business would grow in value. Growth in value is directly proportional to the Profit, so growing Profit grows value.

The amount of Capital thing was an important constraint. Owen realized he had limited Capital and he should risk it wisely.

Several years earlier a man he respected (who had struck out on his own and bought a golf course – oh, how Owen envied him for years!) called early one Sunday morning not to invite him to play golf, but to borrow money. He wanted to borrow a lot of money. He had a "problem." The bank loan was due and he was "a little short". (Funny how the guy who wants to borrow your money is always only a little short and will pay you back real soon!).

Owen lent him the money, but only after getting a lawyer to draw up binding papers (the first of many occasions when an attorney saved his bacon). At the signing, the guy told Owen "I was always undercapitalized – I knew it from the beginning." It's sort of like a pilot who admits, "We always knew we didn't have enough fuel!"

Now, years later, when Owen thought about this story he knew the moral was:

OVER Capitalized = Good

UNDER Capitalized = *Idiot*

He was painfully aware that every penny he had in the world was invested either in CD's to care for his family or in Owen Enterprises (he already had a name for his firm!). That money had been invested in the stock market during the 80's and it was making a pretty good return of 10% or so per year. He wanted to make a return on his Capital – that is the goal of any business, to make a fair return on Capital (look it up; it really is in every book on business).

When he thought about it carefully, he realized he was taking a bigger risk with his Capital in his own firm than he had been taking by investing in P&G, IBM, or Coca-Cola. He believed he should get returns that were proportionate to the risks he was taking. He thought his returns should be greater than 15%. This was very exciting so he opened a bottle of Merlot and announced his goal out loud! The Demons were his only audience, and they just laughed and laughed.

Owen vowed to use his Capital wisely, to ensure that he had enough and to make certain he earned a reward proportionate to the risk he was taking. This would limit what he could do, but he thought he had enough Capital to accomplish his goals.

Then he went to sleep and for the first time in a long while the Demons did not wake him. It turns out that Demons can be controlled by good, sound decisions and then you sleep like a baby (and sometimes after an especially good day sugarplum fairies even show up)!

# 4 STRATEGY
*(This is really, really, really, really important.)*

When Owen woke up the next morning he was, once again, petrified. Sure he had quit his job, counted his money, apportioned it wisely (using great advice), learned he needed to make a handsome return, and made a decision to always have plenty of capital. A lot of hard work had gone into all of this.

But frankly, what was he going to do to make this money? The Demons were amused. They produced accounting statements showing that, thus far, his Profit was negative (bright red in fact), and they harped on the fact that all he was doing was wasting time and money thinking about "strategy." They even made up an inane song he couldn't stop humming:

### *"Where is your paycheck? Where is your paycheck?"*

Incidentally, the Demons never really disappear. No matter what happens, they are lurking like savage wolves waiting for any doubt or uncertainty to crop up. Suddenly there they are – gleefully singing...

### *"Oh yes, you're the great pretender. Pretending ..."*

For whatever reason, during the day Owen was now calm and intense. He had read every business book on startups he could find. Some of the advice was worthless, like:

"Do something unique"

This advice would work well for Steve Jobs, Thomas Edison, and other genius inventors, but it was of little help to mortals like Owen.

Other advice seemed more useful:

"Discover a niche"

A niche product or service is one not many people currently want and, therefore, no other companies pursue, because there is not much money in the niche today. However, it might be a growing need in the future.

Owen spent some time thinking about the niche strategy. He even flew to Chicago to try out a niche offering idea on his best former client (and dear lifelong friend). This client, T, (thinly disguised to protect him) heard Owen out one day over beers at lunch. This was a long time ago when drinking beers at lunch was what you did if you were a responsible professional (all the rest of the business world got ripped on martinis). The screen play and dialogue would go something like this:

EXT. CHICAGO ITALIAN RESTAURANT (no Commies in view)
*Owen and T are seated at an outdoor table talking. Owen is squinting in the afternoon sun.*

    Owen: "So T, I'm thinking I should have a niche for Owen Enterprises and my idea is to specialize in consulting among the aging population of consumers – folks 60 and over and ..."

*T's body language and tone indicate he is dismissive of the idea and thinks Owen is wasting his time.*

    T: "That's a great idea Owen, why don't you call the firm Geriatrics R Us? Can I get another beer? No, actually I want a double martini."

    Owen: "You don't think specializing in work on the fastest growing segment in the universe is a good idea!!?"

*BAM. Owen, pissed at T, slams his beer down on the table, which is precariously balanced on an uneven slate tile floor. The table rocks like there has been an earthquake and a full pitcher of beer gushes over the two of them — all suited up.*

*T calms down after his martini is served.*

T: "Why don't you just do what you used to do for me? You were really good at that!"

This was brilliant advice but the alcohol-induced haze Owen was enjoying caused this thought to be lost for some time. It did resurface later, but T never got full credit — until now.

Owen caught his flight home (smelling like a beer distillery, which the other passengers seemed to notice with disgust), all the while thinking dark thoughts about T. All his hard work on a niche had gone to waste and he would still wake up tomorrow without a strategy.

Hundreds of hours and conversations later he was still frozen with fear. Nothing had happened (other than the fact that all the Demons now had names and some very irritating offspring). He just kept spinning and could commit to a strategy.

Months passed, no money was coming in, and all he had done was talk to bankers, accountants, lawyers, competitors, and old friends on the client side like T (most of whom drank less at lunch, at least). Tired, alone, and frightened, he turned on the word processing program he used in those days to have a conversation with his only ally – the Toshiba laptop.

He typed some fateful words:

1.  It's time to do something! (Owen was proud of this sentence – it seemed like progress). Like a flowing river, this led immediately to:
2.  I should do something I know how to do! (I swear this is a completely true story with no dramatic embellishment). The next sentence was completely obvious to Owen.
3.  The only things I really know how to do are things someone has paid me to do in the past (Thanks, T!).

"Wow," he thought, "What am I really good at? What types of things do I love doing?"

Excited, he retrieved his old records from fifteen years of work with Billie Enterprises and began to carefully document all of the consulting projects with which he had ever been involved. There were about 1,500 of them. It was tedious and time-consuming. But in the end, he discovered a niche he loved and, apparently, as T had said, one that he was good at.

The good news was that the competition sucked at this type of work, and Owen thought it was a growing niche. The really good news was that his Capital was more than adequate to tackle this strategy. Sadly, he forgot T was mainly responsible for all of his future success. (Note - alcohol is a Demon too!).

That was it. He had Capital and a strategy. The Demons were in full retreat (at least for one night). Owen knew what he was going to do.

# 5 NOW OWEN ENTERPRISES
## IS OPEN FOR BUSINESS

Oddly, the terrifying nights were not yet over, because there was no sign of any revenue. He sent announcements to all the prospects he could think of – nothing happened. No sign of Peter Profit, no clients, no employees, nothing. The phone was not ringing. Fortunately, no one had invented video games for office computers yet, and, being afraid of heights, Owen was not tempted to take a flying leap. So he spent all of his time trying to remember how to stir up business.

The Demons had a couple of parties; Owen lost sleep and couldn't find a golf game at the country club. Even his two-year old at home was beginning to think the old man was a loser.

Owen made a list of every single contact he had ever had on the client side of the business – a total of 165 names of people he knew who might plausibly be a potential source of revenue. He ranked them in order using 3 variables:

1. Total budget they had influence upon.
2. Likelihood they would call him back.
3. How happy he would be if they did (real jerk = 10%, sweetheart of a guy = 100%).

By multiplying these numbers together and ranking the prospects on the total, he prioritized his prospect list.

Then he remembered what Bob Salesguy, the wise, old sage from Billie Enterprises who had sent him to England and taught him how to build a business, always said, "Call people who have budgets for your services, take them to dinner (buy fine wine!), and beg for a chance. Really beg – on your knees, tears in your eyes – promise the moon, show pictures of the adorable children (by this time there were two, including a real cute little girl). Just beg for a chance."

And so he did. He got on planes, and did the begging in person (begging on the phone is pathetic). Fly, fly, fly. Spend, spend, spend (it turns out the Demons fly with you and really have a ball on road trips).

Beg, beg and really, really, really, beg. Then he would rush back to the office to sit close to the phone (in those days they had to be plugged in using stupid wires so he actually had to sit in the office hoping some client would call).

Still nothing – no luck (but notice the Preparation). The Demons were having a field day. More than once he started to call the old boss to see if he could rejoin the team.

One day the phone did ring. It was JS – an old friend and former client from a Fortune 500 firm. He told Owen about a problem he and his firm had, and they had a long talk about alternative ways of solving this problem.

Owen finally said, "Well, JS, good luck with your problem." Owen thought JS was just picking his brain – he couldn't imagine a Fortune 500 firm would entrust an important project to a one-man band. Normally they wouldn't, but JS loved Owen, wanted to give him a shot, and had the authority to do whatever he wanted.

Then Owen heard the most astonishing sentence anyone had ever said to him.

"Jeez, Owen, do you want to bid on this or not?"

It had been so long since he had heard that question, he didn't really know what to say or do, but, fortunately, desperation is an ally.

The proposal Owen wrote stands as his best work ever (there is nothing comparable to the terror of losing everything you have in the world as a source of motivation). He sent it off and then raced back to the office to sleep by the phone in case JS wanted to discuss some aspect of it at six o'clock in the morning (that was silly since JS never woke before nine o'clock). Finally, thirty-six long hours later, the phone actually rang and Owen Enterprises was awarded its first project!

Owen immediately opened some Merlot and summoned the Demons (silly, actually, since it turns out the Demons never expect an invitation, they are always there just waiting) and bid them farewell for good. Owen thought the hard scary work that excited the Demons was done. The sad truth is that the hard scary work is never done and the Demons are always there just waiting.

# 6 CASH = OXYGEN

The next morning, Owen arrived at the office and constructed a "To Do List." Because he had no staff, the list was long, including such things as:

1. Write the project plan.
2. Find subcontractors to do their part of the contract.
3. Visit Staples to buy Post-it Notes, pens, a stapler etc. (there really wasn't anyone to delegate anything to at this point).
4. Take out the trash.
5. Go to the school play tonight.
6. Get a haircut.
7. Call Mom.
8. Go to FedEx to pick up envelopes and try to figure out how to use them.
9. Send a bill to JS.
10. Hire someone to do parts of the job I am not equipped to do (the vast majority of the work, actually).
11. Shave at some point today.
12. Coffee.
13. Computer lesson today at 10:00.
14. Lunch with George.

You get the idea. In any new job the "To Do List" is essential. You really don't know how to do the job yet, and it's important to figure out your new priorities. It's like having your first child. It turns out "feed the baby" takes priority over everything else and babies come equipped to "help" you understand this. Did you ever try doing anything else when the kid was hungry?

Owen was born to run a company and he proved it to himself that very morning. Item #9 on the list was a clear cut #1 priority (and honestly, it was at least that far down the list). Cash is to a business as oxygen is to your body. (Owen used to say "as blood is to your body," but you can survive even a very nasty wound for a lot longer than you can hold your breath!)

He created his very first invoice that morning, rushed to FedEx (Oxygen, remember) and paid to send the invoice for $37,500 to an actual Fortune 500 company!!! Hanging out with bankers was beginning to rub off on Owen.

When he checked this item off the list, Owen thought about what to do next, but his mind would not let go of the oxygen thing. What else could he do about cash?

"Ring! Ring! Ring!" JS's phone in Atlanta was ringing.

"Hello?" JS said in a slightly annoyed tone because he had not had his morning Coke yet. It was way too early to be calling JS.

"JS, it's Owen. I just sent the pre-bill to you, ahh, ahh, okay?" Owen knew it was okay, but still couldn't believe Owen Enterprises had an actual Receivable.

"Yeah, sure, of course, you know that," said JS, still annoyed. Then came some deadly words, "But you should know we are notoriously slow payers."

Owen had done business with JS for years but when you work for a huge company the Accounting department pays attention to the "shit work" like that – not the cool Executives. So Owen had no idea about the payment policies of any firm for which he had ever worked. This may be one reason larger companies are so messed up.

"JS, is there anything you can do to speed it up?" Owen asked desperately.

"Well, my assistant loves chocolate candy – maybe you could send her a note and ..." (JS is a sweetheart of a guy.)

"Done!" Owen shouted. He hung up hastily, rushed out of the office, bought some fine chocolates, wrote a sweet note to Kim, the assistant, and ran back to FedEx (Oxygen, remember) to send the package!

Three days later the check arrived. A copy of that first check has hung on Owen's wall for twenty-five years. He will be buried with it!

# 7 STICK TO THE KNITTING

Tom Peters wrote "A Passion for Excellence" more than thirty years ago and coined the phrase "stick to the knitting." He believed that successful firms stuck like glue to the things they were really good at doing. Owen had read the book and could recite long passages from it. He had attended Tom Peters' seminars and actually once shook his hand. When he started Owen Enterprises, Owen was "sticking to the knitting" – doing something he knew how to do.

Except for one tiny little thing.

He knew about clients and problems and designs. He knew how to make the promises it took to win the work.

Keeping the promises requires the work of talented staff. In his world that involved at least three sets of specialized talents, and, while he could "sub-contract" two of these, the third needed to be done in house (or else Owen would have to quickly learn how to be a world-class Project Manager).

Project Managers are kind of like wedding planners. They have to be on top of dozens of details, and be exquisite planners (one who builds a plan and then has contingency plans for problems that probably won't happen). Letter-perfect attention to detail is required. Patience is essential. Meticulous, tidy, and organized are common characteristics of outstanding Project Managers.

Owen had strong leadership, analytic, and strategic skills but attention to detail, shall we say, was comically, tragically and fatally absent. Case in point: in the span of the three years after the advent of cell phones, Owen lost four of them. Literally dozens of personal possessions ranging from briefcases, suits, cashmere sweaters, wallets, and a passport have all been left in hotels. He has flown to the wrong cities on the wrong days. He has "misplaced" (his description) rental cars. The list is enormous.

Owen had won a project, but a strategically critical asset was absent from his roster (it was sort of like not having a quarterback before the Super Bowl). In short, Owen Enterprises had another crisis.

The recently dismissed Demons returned and had a field day. "We told you so!" seemed to be their favorite refrain.

Owen was again in despair and an urgent solution was required. "But who," he mused, "would join a firm that had only been in existence for four months and had yet to complete a project?"

Oh, one other small thing, Owen was taking no salary and was not prepared to pay a salary (it would be accrued in the hopes that it could be paid in the future). Who would take this job? Clearly no one in their right mind!

After a short funk, Owen realized that he had joined a firm – his own – that had even less going for it on day one than Owen Enterprises had right now. Why? Frustration with the old job and Billie Enterprises! And he wasn't the only one who had felt that way about Billie Enterprises; he remembered the TRAITORS who had already left. Maybe someone still at the old firm could be enticed away.

"Enticed" sounded a little sinister. To entice you have to tempt with something and for all of human history, money is the undefeated champion in the enticement arena. How many conquistadors returned with money? Damn few, but thousands were enticed to try it.

The newspapers of 2012 are full of comments about the 99% who are upset about the amount of "stuff" the 1% have. Fully two-thirds of the 1% are business owners. All of them will tell you that they started their firm for every reason under the sun other than money. All of them are being politically correct and hiding the awful truth. Of course it was the money – the same reason Spaniards, by the thousands, sailed to the new world. Gold fever – it's an official disease. Today this venal human addiction to money is politically incorrect and banned from polite conversation.

Owen blames Michael Douglas (as Gordon Gekko in *Wall Street*) for this. Gekko managed to voice a perfectly sensible sentence:

"Greed ... is **Good!**"

in a sinister manner that smeared greed for good.

Owen believed Greed was good (his personal anthem is "Money, Money, Money" by ABBA!). Everyone wants "stuff." Everyone wants houses, cars, computers, Caribbean vacations, and BMW's. Greed creates an appetite for risk and risk is the first cousin of reward. Where would we be if no one took risks?

Owen left Billie Enterprises to found his firm because he thought ownership was a big deal and an important part of that is the moola, cash, bucks, or Euros you would expect to get in return for taking such a big risk.

So Owen started thinking about great Project Managers he knew, making a list of those who had a lot of experience, whom he liked and who seemed to like him in return. He also was looking for someone who was unappreciated at Billie Enterprises.

Owen was going to offer some Ownership. He was prepared to offer 15% of the company to the right person.

The best Project Manager Owen knew from the old firm was a guy Owen had cleverly lost 232 consecutive golf matches to over the prior fifteen years. The guy loved Owen or maybe it was the cash flow he got on the golf course. Owen could sell his ass off and he had a sales job to do. After lots of pleading, begging, and a tiny amount of sobbing, the first hire, Employee #2, said "Yes!" Mainly, Owen thought, because he would get a "piece of the rock!"

Years later, some suggested that Owen had been playing "client golf" to endear himself to #2 (nothing makes fast friends on a golf course like a loser who pays his bets).

The evidence to support this is not compelling.

Employee #2 subsequently played 500 or so matches with Owen over the next 25 years and lost just one time. Owen had no future on the senior tour. He probably could not have made money on the blind tour either. He could, however, be very persuasive when his life depended on it!

Twenty three years later, when #2 tired of beating Owen at golf, he retired. His investment had paid off handsomely. Turns out, #2 was just as greedy as Owen but only in the best possible way.

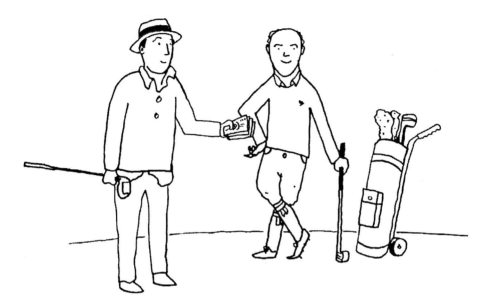

# 8 ENTER THE BARRISTER

In order to sell 15% of the company, Owen needed an Attorney. Shortly after founding the business, Owen had hired an attorney who was a tennis buddy to help him form a corporation. The attorney was a young guy and a very junior associate at the biggest law firm in town. To Owen it seemed like that was plenty "lawyered up" for him and his fledgling enterprise.

By the time Owen wanted to sell 15% of the firm, the young associate had taken a job with a manufacturer and the Owen Enterprises account had been turned over to a senior partner in the largest law firm in the city. The guy was an Olympian (really, he had a bronze medal in swimming) and a graduate of several prestigious Ivy League schools. This seemed like overkill to Owen but it turned out, in the long run, to be the break of the century.

After several abortive attempts to talk Owen out of selling stock in the company (see comments on "No" below), the Barrister drew up the necessary papers, and the sale of stock was consummated. The Barrister was Owen's age and a clever guy who, over the coming years would become very familiar with Owen's firm and his "unique" business practices and personal style.

On virtually every occasion when an issue came up, the Barrister would listen carefully, ask a few questions, and then say, "Let me talk to (insert name of specialist at his firm who had, like, 84 years of experience in this obscure part of the law) and I'll get back to you."

Over the course of the next 25 years, Owen had occasion to work with dozens of talented attorneys who worked for this very large and impressive firm. Tax, employment, immigration, real estate, aviation, divorce (ouch!) and other specialists gave very valuable advice to Owen on numerous occasions.

One day Owen, after yet another panic-stricken call to the Barrister (there is something about a pending legal issue that raises the stakes every time), heard the now customary response. Owen said, "Every time we have a problem and I call, you say the same thing. What exactly is it that _you_ do?"

By that point, Owen realized the Barrister had come to know and understand the business practices of the firm perfectly. He always thoroughly and perfectly briefed the topic experts before the meetings so they were very efficient. Much excellent work was done, much time was saved and, as we all know, these folks bill by the hour. (All attorneys are long winded – really, it's Darwinian.) The very expensive Barrister tapped experienced experts in all areas, and then thoroughly briefed them on the issues so they could quickly craft a solution. This process saved Owen money every time something came up.

Most importantly, however, the Barrister cleverly learned how to get Owen to listen carefully no matter what the issue was. Think about it – if you're talking to an attorney it's because someone somewhere might sue you. You should be careful. Owen was, as previously mentioned, anything but careful. The Barrister soon mastered a sentence that caused even Owen to pause before acting on something that involved a serious legal risk. It went something like this:

"You could do that, Owen, and it might work but it's also possible that you will lose everything you have. Then your children will hate you, the Demons will settle in for the long run and you will have to live on the streets – sort of like Steve Martin at the end of "The Jerk", when he was lying in an alley with a really cheap bottle of wine." The Barrister was a natural born salesman!

Owen likes to share four further observations on Lawyers:

1. They always say "No." It's sort of like having a Marine for a father (without the expletives). It's their job to tell you all the absolutely awful things that might happen if you do this thing you really, really want to do (and probably will do no matter what they say). In some ways they are like all the awful warnings you hear on drug commercials, "In some isolated cases, taking Blgdz has been associated with spontaneous human combustion ... but it will cure the pain of your hang-nail!" Mostly you should let Lawyers moderate or shape the next steps to minimize risks. For example, if "spontaneous human combustion" is plausible, perhaps you should keep a fire extinguisher handy.

2. Despite #1 above, always call the Lawyer **before** you do something that might raise issues. The Barrister repeatedly assured Owen he was unique in that regard (most people apparently do something that gets them in trouble then the call an attorney to bail them out) and, as a result, no legal issues ever really exploded.

3. Lots of impressive names on the letterhead are important. Trust me. The absolute first thing the Barrister does when someone threatens Owen is check out the other guy's law firm. Lots of attorneys and impressive names on the letterhead are as important to success in the legal arena as having a good offensive line is to a football team. Owen's law firm had a former President of the USA and a descendant of a signer of the Declaration of Independence on the letterhead. In "Lawyerland" (mainly refined and polite Ivy League gentlemen) the letterhead is sort of like the aircraft carrier the US sent to the Persian Gulf when Iran threatened its neighbors – a very

threatening group of "gentlemen" with whom to go to war.

4. No individual attorney has all the expertise you might need somewhere down the road. Find a big firm, develop a relationship with a generalist you respect, and don't worry too much about their billing rates.

# 9 GET THE JOB DONE RIGHT

Now Owen had a co-owner possessing essential skills, a client, and a timeline. Nevertheless, the Demons reappeared and made a list of the three hundred assets and fifty years of experience his former employer had that Owen lacked. "No way, José," was the theme of the evening. "Sure, your golden tongue talked JS into a pity sale, but once you screw this baby up and the word gets out (and it always does get out) you can kiss this fruitcake idea of yours goodbye," they exclaimed gleefully.

It is fair to say that no project in the history of the industry got more loving, tender attention from more experienced people than the initial project for JS. Plans were made and refined and remade and refined again. Think Monet and his 25-year obsession with water lilies.

Phase one involved having sub-contractors "gather data" in five cities. Owen and #2 drove to the cities to ensure that the sub-contractors thoroughly understood their needs. They also showed pictures of their families and adorable children to the middle-aged ladies who gathered the data and emphasized they would probably have to put the kids in foster care if the project did not go well.

Once the data was gathered (#2 was a whiz at this stuff so it was perfect!) a data tabulation firm tallied it and gave Owen the "numbers." Owen spent every waking moment for the next ten days using the only technical skill he had to analyze the numbers. These were a lot of waking moments because the Demons were all over this, and sleep was hard to come by. When he was working, the Demons disappeared.

Then Owen Enterprises hired a graphics firm to create a stack of colorful 35mm slides, which was very unusual at the time. The slides were very expensive and not expected by the client. This has come to be called the "Wow!" factor.

JS loved it. JS's internal team loved it. The results were interesting enough that Owen was invited to present to JS's boss, PhD. He loved it and invited Owen to present to the Board of Directors. Even they loved it! Owen was in the Major Leagues! More work was promised and soon materialized.

PhD was an ambitious and brilliant businessman. He would go on to take four different jobs at increasingly larger firms with more and more sizable budgets. PhD and his various staffs subsequently awarded millions of dollars worth of work to Owen Enterprises.

Obsessive attention to detail and delivering a "Wow!" factor will always pay off. Infused with the glow of praise and the promise of more work, Owen hit the road and landed five more projects by the end of the year. In addition, three more new employees were hired. Owen Enterprises was off and running.

# 10 THE FORMULA

It was December – the end of the year. Everyone at Owen Enterprises was beaming at me (Peter Profit). I was tiny then, but they say it was just like looking at your first born child. Owen briefly took up smoking Churchills, the massive cigars favored by Sir Winston, and the cheap Merlot was, thankfully, a thing of the past. The firm had a total of five employees who were now being paid a salary, and Owen thought they should pay a bonus to everyone!

Owen struggled with two things. First, how much of the profits to put in the bonus pool everyone would share? Second, how much bonus to pay to each member of the staff, including himself? It was kind of a weird problem – how much bonus do you pay yourself?

He obsessed over this question and ran hundreds of simulations using a spreadsheet, which was at that time a new and very powerful tool. He was going to get the largest bonus no matter what. He deserved it and in any firm in America that is correct. "It's the American way!" he said out loud.

The Demons showed up and whispered, "Just keep it all – remember, as you always say, Greed is Good! Keep it all, keep it all for yourself – think about the wine you can buy!" It sucks when Demons turn your own words on you for the wrong reasons. The Demons are never your ally, and they are always trying to trip you up.

So Owen began to imagine he was employee #2 or #3 or #4 or #5. All of them, he realized, had taken outsized risks and thus deserved outsized returns. It's a law — great rewards are required when great risks are taken and pay off. He tried to imagine them taking their bonus checks home to their families. Owen had a vivid imagination and he was able to glimpse the reactions of the families if better-than-expected bonus checks were received. The staff would return to the office determined to taste that elixir again.

Owen ran simulations of various scenarios that took money from his bonus and moved it into the pool for the other employees. He quickly realized that their appreciation of and positive reaction to even small amounts of additional money was greater than his feeling of loss. He continued playing with this. As he moved more money away from him and his family toward the staff and their families, the Demons got quieter and quieter. It was cool and surreal. For one manic moment he moved his entire bonus to the employees. Owen became deeply depressed when he contemplated getting no bonus. That would be bad! He worked hard to find a balance point. In the end he got a bonus that thrilled his family, and the bonus paid to the staff thrilled and surprised them and their families as well.

He realized he was actually observing a real-life, real-time example of diminishing marginal utility – the amount of money he was taking out of his pocket still left him a very satisfying bonus. He would get more in the long run in morale, motivation, and commitment from the rest of the staff than he was giving up in the short run. This principle would be used over and over and over during the next 25 years and it always worked.

It's called the LAW of diminishing marginal utility for a reason. Like the LAW of gravity it's always there, it always works the same way, and you can count on it. The Demons were deeply depressed and moved away for a time.

Owen learned an important lesson that night. He postulated the four things he had to do to stay in business for at least five years – he called it The Formula:

1. Find a client. Win a project.
2. Hire the staff you need to do the work perfectly.
3. Make a profit.
4. Share the rewards fairly.

Then repeat that over and over and over. It was and is still that simple. Many years later he realized that this was not the Formula for just five years of success. It is:

# The Formula

# 11 AND SO THE BUSINESS GREW & GREW & GREW

The Formula was correct and it became the constant refrain at Owen Enterprises. Owen believed a growing firm offered employees the chance to get ahead and everyone he hired should be an ambitious person. A growing, profitable firm is a healthy firm. What owner of a business doesn't want to see their profits grow? Each of the four steps of The Formula Owen originally developed continued to contribute to the growth of Owen Enterprises, no matter the size of the firm.

**1. Find a client. Win a project.**

This expanded into a more complex plan of action that included a number of activities:

- Hire experienced salespeople who had established relationships with clients. Go see those clients right away to tell them how excited you are to have their old friend, Zebo, on the sales staff at Owen Enterprises and how eager you are to work with them.
- Attend every conference that might be attended by potential clients and exude confidence. Take lots of key salespeople, because what failing company would do that? Take clients who love you to dinner with prospects (a diabolically clever strategy when mixed with fine wine). When the client who loves you is waxing eloquently about your firm, sit back and feign modesty: "Oh, Vivian, you do go on so, you wonderful woman."

- Deliver thoughtful speeches at conferences in hopes of attracting some attention. Oddly, this is a less productive activity than one would think, but Owen liked the attention and loved the sound of his own voice. So he continues doing this, especially when the conferences are in places like Las Vegas or New York.
- Follow fans. When a client who loves your work takes a new job, you hope they remember you and the fine work you used to do for them. You hope the suppliers of services at the new firm are less attentive than you are. We used to wait for our old fans to call us first. This is very bad behavior and we have since, after some self-flagellation, stopped doing it. Now Owen wants us to send a welcome gift basket along with a picture of their old team, and a note saying "Good Luck, we're missing you, and our children may starve unless you call us soon." Wisely, no one will do this, but having set that stake in the ground, Owen finds everyone is more apt to stay in touch with their clients who change jobs.

## 2a. Hire the staff you need.

We happen to be headquartered in a city that has lots of competitive firms in our industry and, frankly, at any given point in time, some of them are struggling (one actually blew up in 2004 which was a huge break for us). We, however, were growing year after year, had a reputation for success, a huge bonus plan, and a pretty wild Christmas party. Resumes from outstanding people appeared like magic in our inbox. The process was remarkable.

    a) We were growing and needed people, so we told our staff to contact old friends and co-workers.

    b) Soon a resume from someone in town appeared. The applicant was interviewed, offered a job and hired.

    c) Shortly after that, somewhere between three and six other highly-qualified people appeared because their former colleague reports "it's great to work here."

Magically, the newly hired employees have friends, co-workers, and acquaintances all over the country who are also working for firms that are not growing. The snowball gets bigger and bigger.

We have tried other methods including help-wanted ads and headhunters (I'm sorry, *executive search professionals*). Neither has worked very well.

## Help Wanted Ads

Responses to help-wanted ads are odd. Something like this happens regularly.

- **Help-Wanted Ad** – Growing Neurosurgical Practice seeks highly experienced surgeon. Applicant must have extensive experience in frontal lobe blah, blah, blah. Plus, excellent Mandarin language skills are required because most of our patients are Chinese.
- **Typical Response** - I saw your ad and I think I am a perfect candidate. I really kneed a job and I LOVE Chinese food plus, I always carve the Christmas turkey in our family.

This is only a slight exaggeration. Our Human Resources VP refuses to run ads because the needle that might be in that haystack will take four man-years to find. By then, the position will have been filled by a former co-worker of our most respected individual in the department that needs the help. A small side benefit of taking this approach to hiring is that the individual who "endorses" someone takes it personally if the new hire doesn't measure up.

## Executive Search

With one exception, our use of search firms has been grotesquely expensive and painful. Their commission of 35% of year-one pay, when added to the seven man-years of actual pay for the many failures turned up by this particular profession, runs well into six figures (Owen curses and throws things when someone suggests that "maybe we could call a headhunter").

Virtually every candidate the headhunters send your way is one step away from being fired and they have a sixth sense for this. They polish up the resume, send it to dear old Herb the Headhunter. He puts some lipstick on the "resume" and then sprinkles some fairy dust over it before sending it to employers desperate for a perfect candidate. The headhunting firms churn these folks - it's like an annuity. It may seem odd but the folks who change jobs regularly have perfected the art of "Interviewing for a Job." Beware!

A salesperson with a Monet-like resume lasted eighteen months. Hours before being fired, he resigned. When asked about where he was going, he launched into a speech, "When I resign I always follow a five-point program of what to do etc., etc."

He had an actual recipe for resigning ahead of the axe! A standard template of steps! He is three jobs down the road since he left Owen Enterprises. If he ever puts as much energy, creativity, and effort into actually doing a good job as he does into planning his next moves, he might succeed somewhere! Sadly, the federal government makes it impossible for anyone to provide accurate feedback when called about work performance, so even Owen's friends who run other firms can't warn him and Owen can't warn them about these "applicants."

## 2b. Do the work perfectly.

It turns out the Klient (Owen insists his employees spell this with a K to remind them Klients are Kings!) gets to decide if it's perfect. Only the Klient. The main parameters begin with:

- Timing, Timing, Timing – All results of work delivered on time may be deemed acceptable. All results of work delivered late are AWFUL.
- Cost – Costs are assumed to be identical to the original quote except for circumstances as follows: _____ (note nothing follows).
- Content – If the results are good news to ultimate end Klients, we are heroes. In all other cases we have earned our keep, but in the end Klients may be somewhat disappointed with the results. Therefore, we should be prepared to do more work, trying desperately to find ways to make the immediate Klient and the end Klient feel good about the project.

There is only one measure of success with a Klient that really matters – repeat business. We try to treat every project for every Klient like the first project for a new Klient. We are trying to win the next piece of work every day.

## 3. Make a profit.

The goal of any serious business is to "make a profit". The making of profits is the proof that the owners know what they are doing. No business owner starts a firm to "employ lots of people" – firms employ people to make profits. Profits create the financial flexibility all firms need to invest in facilities, hire more people and expand and they do all of these things to "make a profit".

Owen never lost sight of this goal and much of our success stems from this overarching vision. Everyone at Owen Enterprises marched to the same drumbeat – make a profit – we were like the great college marching bands you see a half-time of football games. Always in step everyone always knowing where we were headed.

## 4. Share the rewards fairly

Making profits creates the opportunity to "share rewards". This is covered in multiple places in our story because it is so important. Many people think Owen is generous or nice. Nothing could be further from the truth. Owen is clever. Paying a large bonus that is proportionate to the work done ensures enormous effort by the staff and dedicated attention to doing the work perfectly. This creates steady growth in business and accounts for the superior productivity of the staff.

## The Result

The firm started in 1988 and finished that year with $450,000 in revenue and 5 employees. In 2011 we closed the books on our best year ever at over $41,000,000 in sales. Today we employ 140 professionals – Owen Enterprises is a job creating success story. We grew one Klient at a time and one new employee at a time. Every employee we hired who did a good job created jobs for others but our goal was not to hire more people it was and is to create more profits that are shared fairly across the team of people who created them. Then we hire some more people so they can help create more profits!

## 12 NOTHING BEATS EXPERIENCE

The initial employees Owen hired were all people he had known and worked effectively with for years. All had previously worked for Billie Enterprises, which was going through a very tough patch at just the right time for Owen. All members of the initial team were very experienced in their respective disciplines and had been promoted until they were managing people who managed people who did the work. It turns out people with technical skills love exercising them, but are drawn into management for the money.

Management skills among good technical people are as rare as albino skunks. Most don't like doing the job and it shows. Owen paid these employees the base salary they had been receiving for managing groups of people and put them back to work utilizing their actual skills. It became apparent pretty quickly that three important things were occurring:

1. The tasks were completed faster than before.
2. The tasks were done correctly the first time, every time.
3. Everyone was happier doing this work than they had been managing people.

Clients were thrilled with the response time and accuracy. Owen had not anticipated this outcome, but he decided to learn from this discovery and apply it aggressively.

In every department Owen sought the most experienced staff he could find. He paid top dollar and put them "back to work." Morale was great. The cost picture was even better. Under the old system, relatively junior people would be given complex tasks they really were not qualified to do perfectly. Managers (who could do the jobs perfectly) would then check the work or actually redo it. Thus, two people – one cheap and one pretty expensive – would do and then check/redo the work. A single task might take a week and require forty hours of the junior employee's time and fifteen of the senior employee's time.

At Owen Enterprises the senior staffer (assisted by state-of-the-art hardware, software and training) could complete the task in twenty hours over three elapsed days. This was cheaper and faster than the old system with fewer errors and rework. It was a miracle and still works to this day.

The average level of experience Owen Enterprises offered to clients was double or triple the level of competitive firms, who were lulled into believing that entry level staff, which is cheap, can do the job adequately when supervised by the real pros. By this same logic, the retired Hall of Fame pro quarterback, who is employed as an NFL quarterback coach, is thus assumed to be magically able to channel his skills and former brilliance to the 6th round draft choice, whose passing skills were unexceptional against Division II competition. Right!

# 13 RISK TAKING

In a professional services business the biggest risk commonly taken is whom to hire. Fortunately for Owen the firm did not require massive capital expenditure. Over the years Owen hired 31 very, very experienced, expensive sales people. All of them came equipped with impressive resumes and a gold plated list of Klients whom they were certain would leap for joy at the news that their valued consultant had landed a job at a fine firm like Owen Enterprises.

Fifteen of these individuals failed in the end and were made redundant (a cute European term for "fired"). All got generous termination (guilt) packages so they would go quietly into the night. In total, these folks with solid six-figure salaries, and many with headhunter fees on top, have accounted for a grand total of 0.5% of the company's total sales...ever. The cost of these hires in aggregate was nearly equal to the revenue they produced. The Demons cited this as a clear failure by Owen to exercise good judgment. In addition, many of these individuals garnered feedback such as this from other members of the senior staff during the interview day at Owen Enterprises:

- "Pleasant and well spoken. Seems to have a lot of relevant experience but I was concerned about the 5 jobs he has held in the last 4 years."

- "Claims lots of success in areas that are key to us. Presents herself as very confident of success. A little sketchy on details of technical activities."

Here is the deal. One of those individuals commented on above lasted six months with the company and generated no appreciable business – the other one ranks third for the all-time most revenue generated for Owen Enterprises. Every evaluation of every potential salesperson ever presented to Owen had:

1. More positive comments than negative. It's human nature for people to say something nice (think millions of mothers saying "If you can't say something nice ...").
2. Uncertainty. The applicant interview feedback frequently reads a little like financial predictions for stocks. "The market has gone up a lot and could go up a lot more but it could also crash and we could lose everything." Owen found if he demanded a direct answer to the hiring question he mainly got "Probably would hire him, but very concerned about the _____."

It's pretty simple, really. No prospective hire in sales ever looked like a lock to everyone. If Owen wanted to be a decision maker, then he alone had to make decisions and take responsibility for them, knowing there was no way to be sure he was right. That's why he got paid the big bucks. Owen began to try to come up with a probability of success for applicants to guide his decision making. He kept track of the high and low "success probability" scores he assigned to applicants he hired and then kept track of the outcomes. Note how useful the table below is now for decision making for new hires.

| | Ultimately Successful | Fired |
|---|---|---|
| High Score | 90 | 85 |
| Low Score | 60 | 60 |

The stupid chart above illustrates the problem when hiring prospective experienced and expensive revenue producers – it's a total crapshoot. Owen came to understand he had two choices:

1. Realize that the success rate is unlikely to be much better than 50% and he cannot unerringly pick the winners from the losers so hire no one.

2. Hire pretty much everyone who seems plausible and watch them carefully to weed out the ones who do not fit with the firm as soon as possible.

This was wild. Half of Owens' hiring decisions were planned to be failures but the firm was growing like crazy and the profits kept rolling in. On the other hand, hiring no one (thus a perfect record in the much revered I Never Made A Mistake category) absolutely locks in slower growth, and that would be a failure on a grand scale.

The sixteen successful senior hires have accounted for over 40% of the firm's revenue. Owen was warned by one or more colleagues to avoid hiring each and every one of them. The cost incurred by hiring ultimately unsuccessful senior executives is more than paid for by the success enjoyed from hiring those who do succeed.

Owen came to realize that an executive who brags he never makes a mistake in hiring is actually making them by the dozens – by not hiring all the imperfect-seeming hires who could make a substantial contribution if given the chance. This executive is simply not taking enough risks and should be made redundant, replaced by an executive with some cojones!

Owen now regards all of his "mistakes" as brilliant decisions that helped him find many of his best people. The mistakes were a cost of doing business. No successful entrepreneur is done taking risks - ever.

# 14  GROW YOUR OWN

Owen was a fine salesperson and loved the challenge of landing work. He was eager to grow the firm and soon realized that, after he had landed a large volume of work, he had no time for selling and growing the firm. He had to figure out how to get the work done in a way that would allow him to go get more work. This was especially urgent because in its second full year of business, Owen Enterprises was doing over 80% of its volume with one Klient – a dangerous level of dependence on a single account.

Employee #2, initially hired for his project management skills, had developed a fine relationship with this important client, and gradually #2 took on more and more of the client relationship responsibilities. He soon began to demand "sales credit," which was clever of him since the bonus for the sales function was typically much higher than it was for any other activity in any firm.

Owen balked turning this responsibility over, but he soon saw if #2 really could manage the relationship, then Owen could do what he really wanted to do – chase new business so the firm was not so dependent on one client. In truth, Owen was happier on the road with prospects (drinking fine wine in 5-star restaurants to boot) than he was in the office grinding through the myriad details that needed to be perfect. He and #2 worked on a template the firm still uses today:

1. Whenever there was bad news to convey to the client, Owen placed the call.

2. Whenever there was good news to convey, #2 was the go-to communicator.
3. When new big stuff came up, both guys were all over it.
4. But #2 did the majority of the follow up work.

In no time at all, the key initial client came to prefer to speak to #2! Meanwhile, Owen kept chasing and landing new work from other clients.

Soon, following the same script, other eager new employees who had terrific consulting skills but no real appetite for the degrading begging for business Owen seemed to love, were worked into lead roles with new accounts.

This track record of teamwork became a central plank in the recruiting Owen did to build the team. Bright young potential stars were lured by the prospect that Owen, a superstar salesman, would help them land business and run interference for them for several years but then get out of their way as they took on more and more responsibility. They then earned fine bonus payments. Eventually more than fifteen individuals hired in as support staff became salespeople, and they have accounted for 60% of the total revenue in the history of the company.

This model also proved instrumental in another very important way. Over the next ten years of Owen Enterprises' history a number of key people left the firm:

- One tragic, too-early loss of a beloved partner to cancer.
- The retirement of two senior partners who by the age of 60 decided to play golf full time.
- The too early departure of another (who oddly decided being a world-class mother was more important than making a lot of money).
- A much beloved partner decided getting her PhD and teaching college students in a related field offered her the rewards she needed.
- The retirement of #86 to spend more time with her teenage boys and to pursue her passionate interest in health coaching including nutrition, exercise and food preparation.

In all cases a variation of the early model was used. Junior staff was worked into the accounts long before the departure. They took on more and more responsibility as the senior member slowly backed away. The Good news/Bad news policy was consistently followed. In no case did the firm lose an account. This protocol has helped Owen Enterprises retain accounts even as senior staff retired or moved on to other challenges in their lives.

# 15 THE BANKER

Every business needs a bank and when Owen started the firm he interviewed several different candidates. Initially, Owen, who thought he knew nothing about running a business, assumed some secrets were known by people like bankers, accountants and lawyers – kind of like a treasure map to profits. Sadly, that is not true. All of the candidates he talked to could provide useful advice, but in the end it was up to Owen and his team to find the treasure.

The personal advice about funding the family and the business which was described earlier remains the most valuable contribution ever made by a Banker. Bankers live in a world of suspicion, worry, and doubt. Maybe they have been left holding the bag so often by silver-tongued devils that, like the cops of this world, they simply believe we are all lying all the time.

Owen once asked a cousin who was a State Trooper (and a very good one) why cops' friends were always cops. He explained, "Everyone else lies to us all the time – we begin to be disgusted with everyone."

When Owen challenged this seemingly cynical view of people, his cousin memorably replied, "I only had one beer ... I was only going 35 ... I didn't know my plates were expired ... etc. etc. etc." Bankers apparently have the same opinion of pretty much everyone.

Bankers like two things – cash (it really has the same effect on them as drugs do on junkies) and a thing they call collateral. Collateral is broadly defined as anything the borrower has that the bank could confiscate and then sell to someone else (your kids are not collateral). If you pledge collateral, they will lend you money, but as soon as they leave your office the Banker Demons (a very terrifying pit bull like breed who come out in the daytime) crowd into the back seat and start snarling and growling and snapping at them. The Banker gets back to his office in fifteen minutes and calls to ask, "How's business?"

Owen, like all business owners, hangs out with other business owners (think "support group"). The ones whose businesses require capital equipment or inventory have collateral, thus Banks will lend them money at high interest rates and on very demanding terms. As soon as the money is lent, the banks become terribly interested in getting all of their money back real, real, real soon.

Get a bank; get a good and big one. Be nice to them - pretty much like you treat the maiden aunt you like who might mention you in her will. Bankers are nice people and their professional behavior is something they can't help.

The old saying that banks "are always ready to lend you money until you need it" is true – literally true. If you ever get in a jam and think to borrow money from a bank to bail the firm out, it's time to find a buyer for the firm. In fact, it's probably too late.

# 16 THE ACCOUNTANT

Owen's first accountant probably spoiled him for the ones that followed. Big Daddy, as his fraternity brothers called him, became a close friend and a teacher/advisor until he callously took a very important job (for a lot more money) and left his practice, leaving Owen in a funk for years. Since then, several very fine professionals have rendered valuable services, especially in dealing with a tax code no sensible human being would ever purposely try to understand. The corporate tax returns require the felling of one very stout oak tree every year and all Owen ever does is sign them. Notwithstanding this excellent work, no other accountant ever got elevated to Beloved External Advisor Status (only the Barrister and Big Daddy have achieved this rank).

No one really knows how they are going to do when they first decide to "run their own business." Envious non-business owners say it must be great to "be your own boss." All business owners who are honest will tell you it's a nightmare. The business now runs you; the Demons make sure of that. Just try taking a day off to play a round of golf or lay on a beach during the first five years or so. It's like getting in the car to take a long trip and at the one hundred mile mark your wife asks, "You did turn off the gas fireplace, didn't you?" The only rational thing to do is turn around immediately, because otherwise you will live in mortal fear for the next hour before turning around anyway.

Big Daddy would come by at the end of the year and Owen would nervously show him the numbers. Big Daddy would say

"You're doing great. You've made money, and the government is not going to take it all away so you can pay a generous bonus again this year and still have fine profits."

Owen, who was sure that he and the accountant must be missing something, would say (and he is not proud of this) "Liar, liar, pants on fire! We must be missing something because everyone said I'd fail and you're saying we are profitable!"

Big Daddy would then go very patiently through a bunch of jargon like "receivables, payables, depreciation, revenue in excess of billings, excess liquidity, discounted cash flow etc., etc.," while showing endless forms with columns of numbers on them. Beaten into submission, Owen would pay the bonus, sign the tax returns, and cash his checks. It was exhausting for both parties and may have had something to do with the Accountant's subsequent career decision.

Big Daddy mainly taught Owen that making money in a business was not all that hard.

1.  Charge more for your services than they cost to provide.
2.  Pay your taxes.
3.  Keep the rest for:
    a.  Bonus.
    b.  Profits.

Then take a vacation and tell the Demons to "sod off" (clever English expression that means "get lost").

# 17 INTERMISSION

The sun was up and several new customers stumbled into the bar to order coffee. Peter Profit was stunned to see it was morning – he had been talking non-stop. Maybe it's true that they pump oxygen into the casinos in Las Vegas. He couldn't believe he'd been at this for so many hours.

Hewlett Packard Profit sat patiently through the whole monologue, but frankly, it was time for some rest. She asked, "Peter could you come to New York next month to share your whole story at the Aspiring Entrepreneurs Conference that I am chairing?"

Peter asked, "Why would a bunch of people who are trying to start all kinds of businesses want to listen to me? We're only a pip-squeak of a firm and our industry is very specialized. Surely they have nothing to learn from us."

"Peter, I still don't know what Owen Enterprises really does and it doesn't matter to me. You haven't been talking about industry specific events – you are telling a story of how a new firm was born and then grew into a profitable, healthy business. Your lessons are recent and fresh. The old firms were founded long ago, in a completely different environment, and they can't remember what happened. Much of what you have to say would apply to any business," explained Hewlett Packard Profit.

So a date to meet was set. Peter, exhausted and exhilarated, went to bed for a very long sleep.

# 18  NEW YORK CITY

Peter arrived in New York City and after a stroll down Fifth Avenue went to his hotel – a very grand place indeed. He met with the executive board of the Aspiring Entrepreneurs Conference to discuss the meetings. The chairman of the conference welcomed him.

"Peter, thanks so much for taking the time to be here today. Hewlett Packard Profit had great things to say about your conversation in Las Vegas."

Peter hoped she had not mentioned the time, venue, or the three brandies he had consumed.

The chairman continued, "We're sorry Owen couldn't be here, but frankly, it may be better to hear this from you rather than the founder."

"Owen sends his apologies; he was looking forward to this. We had a problem on a project and he is on his way to talk to the Klient and do damage control. Owen is a fanatic about this – he always says the Klient is King – he even makes us spell Klient with a K."

"Klient is King – hmm, I hope you will tell our group a bit about that and anything else you think they might find useful."

"Great – I'll start with that if you'd like."

Peter had never seen so many people in a room. They were young and old; some were well-dressed and some looked like snowboarders waiting for the next lift to the top. He was nervous, but he also knew adrenalin was pounding through his system and that meant he'd be sharp.

Peter looked out into the sea of faces and he was amazed at how intently the audience focused on him. He began to speak.

# 19 THE KLIENT IS KING

When Owen Enterprises first opened we had no Klients, just a dream that started with "Find a Klient." A Klient is not a family member or a friend and they are not simply part of a professional relationship. They are actually much, much more. They are the source of oxygen that we needed to survive.

A Klient is, first of all, a person. We list firms on our Klient list but no one at Owen Enterprises thinks of the firms as our Klients. Klients have names and families and aspirations. Like Gary. Visualize our Klient named Gary. He's a very smart guy in a mid-level position, with big dreams. He's ambitious, hoping to go all the way to the top. He works for a large company, but he's in a small, outpost kind of division. He has the authority to select suppliers of services. He has <u>budget</u>. When a Gary awards Owen Enterprises a piece of work, he is risking his career and professional reputation on us. We treat this as you would if he asked you to look after his newborn baby. That kind of perspective will keep you focused on taking care of the Klient.

Gary has two choices when a project is up for bid – go with some tried and true big firm (no one ever got fired for picking IBM) who will put junior people on his work and treat him like the tiny, insignificant source of revenue he is to them, or find a new, risky start-up that will treat him like a King. Oh, and, incidentally, the start-up will put very senior people who are terrified of failure on his work. Gary, our largest Klient even, actually knew Owen's Demons personally and may have offered them some training seminars to ensure that Owen and Employee #2 stayed "on their toes"!

When Owen first talked about Klients as Kings, he realized many of the younger staff thought of Kings like Juan Carlos of Spain or Prince Rainier or Queen Elizabeth (who honestly is more of a king than the other two). These people are accidents of birth wearing expensive clothes and valuable jewels, standing in the same place their ancestors stood back when Kings had actual power.

Instead, Owen told his staff to think of the King named Longshanks in the movie *Braveheart*. Longshanks returns to England after having ravaged France to find his son weakly trying to explain the chaos in England. His son's lover dares to speak and Longshanks hurls him out the window as casually as someone would remove their hat. A Klient is that kind of King – the off-with-his-head sort.

When we at Owen Enterprises think of our Klients as Kings, we become servants – determined to please them in all ways, and never so impudent as to cause the slightest unhappiness lest we be hurled out the window. These Kings typically have the power of life or death over us, but, generally speaking, they have little real power in their organizations. They don't want us to know that, but we have to understand the dichotomy. Their management simply expects perfection in all things with no fuss, muss, or bother. Oh, and be quite quick about it.

Many protocols at Owen Enterprises have been developed to guide our treatment of King Klient:

1. Gary routinely expected results faster than we could deliver them using conventional solutions. We spent no time arguing with him and simply figured out how to give him what he needed. Timing demands from Gary were always ridiculous compared to what the industry typically could deliver and they escalated every time we met the new impossible time line. Owen once asked Gary why he was always in such a hurry. (Big insight coming here.) Gary explained, "When the CEO asks a question in a busy meeting which then goes on for hours, you have until the next morning, at the latest, to answer the question – otherwise the CEO will forget it was asked, forget who you are, and wonder what you are doing cluttering up the hallway." When we got his stuff done quickly, the CEO learned his name and began to come to Gary for even more stuff. Gary wins, we win.

2. On rare occasions when Owen Enterprises has had undertakings go badly, we have never whined and offered half measures. When we deliver flawed work, we do it over and do not charge for any of the work. No one in our world does this. Our competition thinks they are small and the Klient company – let's say IBM – is big, and they believe the $50,000 will mean nothing to IBM. It doesn't. However, it does make the Garys of our world look incompetent when they have to request more money and that is not a good idea in the long run. Our goal is to make Gary look like a genius – then he will win the promotions he seeks and that always comes with more budget.

3. When something goes wrong on a project, get on a plane, beg forgiveness, pay whatever it takes to fix it, then apologize again. Weep and then flail yourself, even if it was an act of God or a problem actually caused by the Klient. That is where Owen is today – begging for forgiveness and promising the moon to fix the problem IN PERSON (no one cares if you are weeping or bleeding when you are on the phone!)

4. When you do things like pay for the Klient's mistakes, don't act like a martyr. Act like you are ashamed - actually, don't act ashamed - *be* ashamed. Recognize that somehow, someway you could have saved the day. You could have saved their baby. In fact, you are an incompetent fool for not saving the baby.

5. "No" may be a complete sentence and a tune the Barrister sings with energy. Strike it from your vocabulary when speaking to a Klient.

6. If you do all of this, you will create Klients for life because they will know you have their backs.

Gary was a Superstar; he got regular promotions, and then won four more jobs in twenty years with increasing power, responsibility, and budget. Everywhere he went, Owen Enterprises went too. Today we can credit Gary, and the people we met through him, with over 40% of the total historical revenue at Owen Enterprises.

Owen and Gary became fast friends. Gary called one day to say he was stepping down to give something back by teaching in the "worst high school in America" – a lifelong dream of his. Owen loved Gary and was proud of his decision, but thoughtlessly said "That's great, Gary, but what the f*#@ is in it for us?"

In truth he misses Gary every day of his life. The challenges of living up to the most demanding Klient ever made Owen Enterprises the success it is today.

# 20 THE RECEPTIONISTS

I struggled to find the right place to mention this, but Owen said he considered this to be an absolutely essential part of the story and it seems to fit right here, in the "Klient is King" stuff. The Klients call us all the time and we have an actual person who knows them answer the phone. A very old-fashioned solution.

Years ago every company in America had receptionists. Their job description in the HR manual was to answer the phone. "Good Morning/Afternoon, this is Owen Enterprises, whom would you like to speak to?"

Some genius efficiency experts, who know nothing about actual business or actual Klients or actual receptionists, read the job description and decided an automated phone answering system could save a few bucks. So now, today, when you call a service provider you mainly get the following menu:

1. Press 1 if you know your party's extension number (these people are nuts).
2. Press 2 if you recently died owing us money.
3. Press 3 if your Mother abandoned you as a child and you need to talk about it.
4. Press 4 if you have no idea what number to press.
5. Et cetera
6. Et cetera

There is a 95% probability that if you guess right, you will be put into "phone mail purgatory." This is a place where you hear something like:

"Hi, sorry you missed me (for the 50th consecutive time). I am either on the phone (with someone more important to me than you are), in a meeting (with someone more important to me than you are), out of the office (meeting with people more important to me than you are), on a vacation, or possibly dead. Please leave a message at the tone and I will call you back real soon (however, I get to define how long that will be)."

Owen remembered the day when you called a firm and you spoke to a sweet lady who would say (immediately before you had to say your name):

"Hi, Owen, how was your vacation in Aruba?"

"Great, Penny, how about your holidays?"

Okay, sometimes you heard some long tedious stories but you get the idea. They knew who you were and you knew them and you didn't feel like a pain in the ass for calling their firm.

Eventually Penny, who knew everything, would say something like, "I assume you are calling for Randy." She said this because she recognized your voice right away. Randy was the only person you ever asked for, and Penny actually knew this. "He is having a colonoscopy (more details than absolutely necessary but very trusting) this morning but he told me if you called to put you through to Tom, who is minding the store in his absence." It was like calling Mom without the recriminations for not calling since yesterday!

According to Owen the automated phone answering system is the single worst innovation in management since the development of cubicles. A bright and capable receptionist is a much better solution for a service company that is desperate to be responsive to Klients, than the cheaper, automated phone system.

In addition, the receptionist knew everything. Seriously, if you want to know "what is really going on," they are the go-to resource. Owen learned early on that a nice lunch and a little vino would loosen the lips of even the most tight-lipped.

Throw the machine away, hire a personable, bright person, and I guarantee an immediate 10% increase in productivity.

## 21 THE ELEVATOR

A man Owen admired once remarked that a business based on the coordinated efforts of talented people was not for him because the "assets leave in the elevator every night." This smart man vowed to, and did, build businesses that were what he called "protected." Imagine that you developed a miracle drug and got a patent. You could charge whatever you wanted for it. The staff could not produce your drug if they left to join the competition, so they were of no threat to your firm. In this scenario, the people who staff the firm are relatively unimportant and easily replaced.

Owen was no genius (which he proved in thousands of ways every day) and thus had to build and manage a business that relied on the staff working together as a seamless unit. Many of the salespeople had completely independent relationships with their Klients and could possibly take their Klients with them if they left.

The support staff had value in the marketplace and would be quite difficult to replace. If they left, Owen would have serious problems. And they did leave – every single night, every last one of them cruelly got in the elevator and left. The Demons (who never quit, it seems) would screech about this with some regularity. It was sort of like the chorus "Leaving on a Jet Plane/Elevator ..." It was maddening.

Owen knew this was a big problem and he knew it because he (and the TRAITORS) had left Billie Enterprises and taken both work and people with them.

Somewhere Owen had read that every big problem comes with opportunities. So he thought about it for a long time and then (Inspiration!!) he decided to make a list of everything he had ever experienced at prior positions that made him unhappy. He made a very long list.

After exhausting himself on this (the list was very, very, very long and every time he remembered another example of something that seemed wrong he would get pissed off about it all over again – this was an extremely tiring exercise), he decided to try to figure out what he could do to minimize or overcome each item so everyone who worked for him would be eager to get on the elevator again in the morning and return to work. After all, they had to go someplace to work, so why not at Owen Enterprises?

He had to make the elevator as inviting as the entrance to Disneyland! Then his employees would work long hours and still be eager to return.

## The Facilities

Billie Enterprises, where Owen had worked for fifteen years, at one point renovated a big, beautiful "Art Deco" building. The really Senior Executives had offices with paneling and high ceilings. They were palatial.  One even had a fireplace. A handful of other VP's had small offices, but the vast majority of the staff, maybe 95% of the total employees, had cubicles that ranged from small to pathetic.

Honestly, the "walls" seemed to be no more than three feet off the ground. There was no privacy at all. The noise level in some areas was sort of like an airport terminal. Some of these folks were visited by Klients and it was embarrassing. There was room in the cubicle for maybe one visitor. If two or more showed up, everyone stood up like prairie dogs.

If you arrived at work and called your spouse with a snappy rejoinder for the last nasty thing she said to you as you left for work, there was a pretty good chance that people at lunch in the cafeteria would assume a divorce was already in the works. All firms, of course, have rumor mills – the speed with which gossip spreads and how it is amplified/distorted increases exponentially as the space/barriers between people diminish. If you have to call your Doctor during the day (remember this is back when phones only worked if they had wires plugged into the wall) to report that your "movements" were not yet satisfactory, that much-hoped-for invitation to your colleague's Super Bowl party might suddenly disappear.

When Owen Enterprises first rented their own space, it fortunately had no interior walls. Employee #2 worked with builders to create a "warren" (as the designer called them disdainfully having had his nifty cube farm pitched out immediately) of individual offices – offices with walls to the ceiling and doors that could be locked.

In 1990, the cost to build the ten private offices was $120,000. We could have had a couple of offices for the execs and 12 cubes, a total of fourteen "offices," for $108,000. Math (Anybody want to argue with math?) suggests that it cost Owen Enterprises $150 more per person per year to house their employees in a dignified and respectful manner. It is worth noting that this is a tiny percentage of the annual compensation of these professionals.

Those offices are still part of the headquarters office space twenty-five years later. The firm now occupies 60,000 square feet and every single professional in the building (other than the much beloved receptionist) has an office and a door! It is hard to say what amount of dignity and respect this confers on the staff. Staff turnover, which averages 20% per year in the industry, is about 2% per year at Owen Enterprises. This cannot be entirely because of walls and doors but the staff knows they are respected and that is worth a lot.

Fifteen years into Owen Enterprises, Owen was interviewing several applicants from a prestigious university who had been wined and dined by some very large, well-known firms prior to visiting his tiny, unknown, and apparently unimpressive company (their attitude suggested this was what they thought of his much beloved firm). They casually mentioned their wonderful days visiting these Fortune 100 companies in hopes of impressing Owen. He said, and I quote:

"How many people did you speak to during your day at (largest firm on the planet)?"

"I can't really remember – I guess maybe eight."

"How many of those people had an actual office with walls to the ceiling and a door?"

"Oh, gee, maybe one or two."

"Wow, who were those folks?"

"Well, obviously, the most important!" (Owen knew this was going to be the answer but the applicant said it as if Owen might be slightly dim-witted.)

"How many of the – let's see (looking at applicant's list as if he didn't know the answer) eight – people you interviewed with here today had an ACTUAL OFFICE, WITH AN ACTUAL DOOR???"

(Meekly, now that they saw where this was leading) "All of them?"

"Yes, and that is because all of them are _____?"

The previously arrogant, recent graduate now humbly, and hopefully in awe, answers, "Important?"

Every mission statement since the beginning of time claims somewhere "people are our most important asset." The average fifth grader can tell if you think they are important. Putting important adults in cube farms tells every one of them, right away, that management is lying. The claim that this fosters open communications and teamwork is false. It robs everyone of dignity and eliminates the ability of managers to readily deal with simple problems with grace and sensitivity in a timely manner. Owen read *Dilbert* every day to make sure we did not do any of the stuff the Boss did that robs people of their dignity, pride and morale.

## My child/mother/aunt is ill

When Owen was a new father during his days as an employee at Billie Enterprises, his three month old first-born son contracted spinal meningitis. Great doctors, a fine children's hospital, and prompt responses turned this possible tragedy into a two week hospital stay for Baby W. Owen spent the first night (and the second and third) holding his child, who had a dozen wires and tubes attached to him, all night long. By the fourth day Baby W was doing fine, but needed to stay in the hospital for ten more days. Owen thought he should maybe go to work (all the nurses voted for this option as well!). When he got to work, he wondered what the hell he was doing there, so he immediately returned to the hospital.

For two weeks, until Baby W. went home, he stayed at or near the hospital. No one questioned what he had done or why. By now, late in his tenure at Billie Enterprises, a lot of people had heard he was "erratic" and kind of steered clear. He "got away" with doing the right thing, but in most firms in America this sort of behavior would not be permitted or tolerated for anyone.

Years later, when events similar to this occurred at Owen Enterprises, he sent staff members home to take care of their responsibilities. He knew from personal experience that in these situations, there were no good choices. Attend to a loved one (while worrying about work), or stay at the office and worry about a loved one while going through the motions at work.

This seemed like a very simple decision. If an Indy Car driver is momentarily concerned about his sick child who is in a hospital, then perhaps driving 230 mph in a race is a bad activity choice. Doing Gary's work perfectly requires absolute concentration and no one could be expected to put that first and foremost in mind when their child is in the hospital.

From the beginning, when someone had a personal crisis (they and only they get to decide if they have a crisis), they were required to get out of the car (figuratively speaking) and go home. Others covered their work. We all expect to cover for co-workers who face such situations and know full well that they will cover for us in return. We are not a family, but we are a team!

## How are we doing?

Owen found that starting from scratch – a one man firm – with a blank sheet of paper presented an amazing "zero base budget" sort of mentality, in real time. Every sensible human being who is employed by a firm of any kind worries about the health of the firm – every single one of them. Most firms are not always (ever??) honest with their employees. When Owen was a one-man band, all of his staff knew how the Enterprise was doing. When it was good, Owen was proud and happy. When it was struggling, Owen was tense and determined to get back to feeling proud and happy.

In the early days, the entire staff, who could easily fit in a small booth at the local diner, would meet every Monday morning to review the previous week and apportion work. Communication – lots of honest communication – took place. Everyone left the Monday Morning Meeting fully aware of the current situation.

As the firm grew, adding more staff and offices, there always had to be a space in the building for a Monday Morning Meeting. The agenda has changed over time to suit the scale, but it always includes Owen standing in front of the team, all of whom have a copy of the Weekly Report in their hands. The Weekly Report provides a comprehensive summary of results year-to-date – Sales, Pending Sales, Sales by Klient, etc., which are all contrasted with both annual goals and results from the previous year. It is sort of like the Sunday paper showing the standings in baseball and a summary of individual stats. Your average child, with a thirty minute training session, could easily see "how the firm is doing." Seeing this information has the exact effect on the staff as it has on Owen – during good times the staff is proud and happy and during difficult times they become tense and determined to get back to the good times.

Owen has hired many experienced professionals over the years and they have commonly expressed amazement at this practice. "I know more about Owen Enterprises after a single half-hour meeting than I knew about how we were doing at my previous firm, ever!"

We actually respect our staff and treat them like mature, responsible adults. They like that a lot, maybe even more than having offices with walls and doors.

## Free snacks

When the firm first moved into what is now the office building we own, we had five employees and there were no restaurants nearby or vending machines in the building. It was an older building with only one other tenant, but in a convenient part of town and importantly ... dirt cheap.

Since Owen drank lots of coffee, a coffee service was essential. Employee #2 did not drink coffee, preferring tea and soft drinks. Tea was also stocked and soft drinks placed in the refrigerator. Oh, and since having a beer was a pleasant Friday afternoon ritual, some beer was stocked for "beer thirty" (4:30 on Friday afternoons). Nothing goes with beer like popcorn, nuts, or chips so they, too, were stocked.

At some point, Owen, who really didn't like eating crackers, chips, or popcorn, "suggested" that some fruit be added. Soon there were soft drink machines on every floor, snacks everywhere, fresh fruit every week, and it was all free!

This may not have been the best idea in the history of ideas and may be a warning to all of you who are thinking of starting firms. If you start something like this, it is sure to grow (at one point the snack cupboard would have done the average convenience store proud!). Undoing this is sure to be more trouble than it is worth, so to this day, Owen Enterprises continues to provide this benefit.

## The Annual Party

At the end of the first year, five couples gathered at the finest restaurant in town and celebrated the fact that oxygen was flowing. A handsome bonus had been paid and the prospects for the next year looked great. It was a very nice and memorable occasion.

Four years later, the firm booked a riverboat for what were now the annual festivities, with open bar, great food, and fine wine. There was lots of dancing and merry-making. The date of one of the staff was her ex-husband. She had not been able to secure an alternative escort so she invited her still- bitter ex. She looked great and flirted with all of the available men. The ex-husband drowned his sorrows with a very large quantity of free adult beverages. At the end of the evening, once we were back on shore, he roared out of the parking lot spinning the tires of his red Camaro (I am not making this up!).

Owen's blood ran cold, despite his own merry-making indulgence that evening. The guy was in no condition to drive and it was Owen's fault. Owen had a limo for the evening and many others had "designated drivers" or had arranged for cab rides. The Demons enjoyed themselves for the rest of the evening and Owen decided to do something different the next year.

His former firm had once held their annual party at a posh hotel and all of the attendees were given two free drink tickets but no rooms. The senior staff, being flush, bought all the additional very expensive drinks they wanted. The less generously compensated partygoers showed real ingenuity. They really couldn't afford the exorbitant drink prices so (very clever stuff here) they snuck in their own beverages. To Owen, this seemed wrong on many levels.

Owen loves his wine and many other adult beverages. He has on occasion, in the high excitement of a party or celebration, been "over-served." (Seriously, this is what he calls drinking to excess – juvenile but true.) He was determined to have a party, determined to treat all as equals and determined to protect the firm from lawsuits.

The next year, all party attendees were given hotel rooms in the same fancy hotel where the festivities were held. Round-trip cab fares were paid for by Owen Enterprises for all who could not spend the night. This annual party has become famous. It is like prom night for adults! Even the Barrister seems content with this solution!

# 22  CASH IS YOUR FRIEND

Owen had been in sales in his prior life and always looked forward to his annual bonus. Salespeople in all firms report their numbers and frequently these results are published. The "friendly" competition to be the best or in the top 10 seemed motivating to Owen especially since he respected his peers and craved their respect.

For the first couple of years our company was in existence, Owen operated the ever-popular "capricious and arbitrary" bonus system favored by cigar-smoking CEO's everywhere. You go in a room, think about performance, which employee you like the best, and who sucked up the most. Then you write some numbers down on a piece of paper and that is the bonus awarded.

Once at Billie Enterprises, Owen's boss called to tell him his bonus amount. Owen expected maybe $5,000. The firm had managed a spectacular year, unknown to Owen, and the Boss "really liked Owen." (Owen had forced himself to drink beer from long-neck bottles and feigned an interest in country music when dining out with his boss. This behavior had won Owen "favorite" status. Sorry, that's how it works in most places.) Owen's bonus was $27,500! He was blown away and very excited. Later when he thought about it, he realized it would have been far better if he had known all along this was in the works. He might have produced even more valuable work.

Owen decided that a very large percentage of the available "profits" would be allocated to a bonus pool to incent everyone to do their best to create profits. (Since we are now talking about creating me, Peter Profit, I'd like to offer my thanks to all of them right here!) The employees who contribute the most toward creating profits should get the most in bonus, Owen reasoned, and they should know it is coming. The question was how to accomplish that.

Employee #4, was a brilliant, articulate and independent-minded Arizona girl who had worked for Owen during his time at Billie Enterprises. Owen gave her the problem of figuring out how to apportion the bonus, thinking this would keep her out of his thinning hair for a while. She did not agree with Owen on all things, and offered painful and well thought-out evidence that Owen might be a Neanderthal – note that this predated the entertaining GEICO commercials.

Aided by a very sharp external consultant, #4 returned quite quickly with a suggestion that laid the foundation for a bonus system unlike any we have ever seen anywhere. In business schools for a time, the mantra "clear line of sight to the bottom line" was presented as a way to motivate employees. The learned academicians never actually laid out how management was to achieve this goal, but lots of PhD dissertations got excellent marks for the cool idea. The notion was if every employee could "see" the impact of their efforts on the corporate profits, that would make them rush back to the hot, nasty cubicle to do or die for dear old Bullship, Inc.

#4 agreed that it was nice to know your efforts had a positive impact on the bottom line of the firm but this was not the same as actually being personally rewarded for those impacts. She reasoned that getting some of the gold you produced might be just the trick. If "Greed is Good" for entrepreneurs and causes productive efforts in them, then perhaps it would work for everyone. Remember, cold hard cash is the all-time, undefeated champion in the motivation department.

At the time, the staff at Owen Enterprises was divided into five groups:

1. Salespeople who went to see Klients and solicit work.
2. Project Management staff that regularly interacted with Klients to complete the work.

3. Behind-the-scenes number crunchers who were very skilled and hard to find.
4. Analysts who looked after technical areas of the projects.
5. Support staff who manned the phones, made the copies, handled shipping and so forth.

#4 suggested that the entire pot of gold (bonus dollars) could be thought of as a pool to be divided into five smaller pools, one for each functional area. The sales staff should get the largest share of the pool because they had the ability to influence Klients to work with us. The support staff had little direct ability to bring money in, but they deserved a bonus because they often had to work the longest hours and did a number of critical tasks which, if messed up, could cause us to lose a Klient. In fact, the proportionate share of the bonus dollars going to each department should be calculated based on what was called "proximity to the Klient." Owen got very excited about this because he could see a way out of the capricious and arbitrary systems others used.

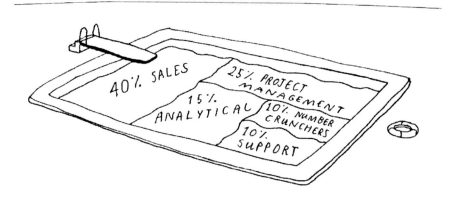

Once the entire bonus pool was divided into the functional pools, it would need to be apportioned to each individual in that area. Owen had already been keeping track of the revenue brought in by each salesperson so it was pretty easy to calculate their "shares." If you sold 25% of the annual total you got 25% of the sales bonus pool.

It also turns out that Owen's system recorded the amount of revenue handled by individuals in groups two through four. One of the women in group two was by far the most productive member of the entire team. She had handled 65% of all the revenue; therefore, she earned 65% of the group two bonus.

Following this logic, the bonus for the highest paid 20 out of 25 staff members had a clear-cut empirical basis! Owen was thrilled.

This approach also lent itself to the single greatest motivational tool Owen has ever seen. The aforementioned Weekly Report at the Monday Morning Meeting shows every department where project responsibility is handled. A $100,000 sale results in 100,000 points in the sales bonus pool for the salesperson, and then 100,000 points in the Project Management pool for the individual who handles it in that group and so forth. These numbers are published every week for all to see. For added emphasis they are trended (last year vs. this year).

At every Monday Morning Meeting, the staff assembles, picks up their copy of the Weekly Report, glances at the first page to see how the firm is doing (if up, bonus will be up; if down, the total pool could be down), and then quickly turns to the department pages to see where they and their friends rank. Everyone wants to be high on this list. Every single employee in the history of the firm could tell you their number and how they are doing this year compared to friends, co-workers, and the stars in their group.

They also look at other groups to see who is really making it happen this year and who is off. The project staff assigned to a slumping sales staff frequently find a way to casually sidle into the sales office to ask, "What's up? What's coming up? And when are you going to get out there and get some oxygen for us???" This made Owen's job easier since motivation (i.e. yelling at salespeople) has always been a key responsibility for management. Now Owen had enlisted the entire staff to assist in this process. (The Demons, upon seeing this diabolical plan, hired a "therapist" and took a long vacation.)

Further, when project managers or other staff members have time unfilled by their assigned salesperson, they have been known to roam the halls, circling like vultures outside the more productive sales teams in search of some spare work they can do. This creates real motivation for salespeople to ensure that they maintain sales levels that will keep their staff busy.

Think about it. Everyone has a clear line of sight to their personal share of the bottom line and that, my friends, will get attention. I, Peter Profit, am the living, breathing result of this energy, determination, and drive.

And now think about the impact this has on the Elevator problem. The bonus paid to the team is highly significant to all of them. It is paid in early December to anyone who is an employee as of that date and as a result no one resigns in mid-year – no one. Everyone understands that the more dollars worth of work they handle, the larger their bonus will be. This makes the Elevator the Portal to Success. The employees come back each morning!

Last and certainly not least has been the completely unanticipated impact of the bonus system on the department heads' perspective on headcount (we hate that word). Let's say a group of ten people in a department were looking forward to a great bonus year. Imagine it's August and the firm is really, really, really busy. People are staying late, working from home, and coming in on Saturdays. In every other firm in America the team manager would be demanding more people. What do you suppose happens at Owen Enterprises?

Many times Owen has had to go to the managers and insist on hiring more staff. All the Department managers push back and say, "We can do this – its fine!" Labor productivity at Owen Enterprises is (are you ready for this?) 40-50% higher than the industry average!

# 23 A PROBLEM WITH BONUS

Owen made the bonus opportunity the centerpiece of his recruiting pitch to prospective new hires. The base wages were industry standard and/or generally what the individual was making in base wages at their current job. Persuading an experienced veteran who was working for a well-established firm to switch to a start-up firm that offered mainly the chance of excellent bonus payments was tough, especially because "bonus" had obtained the reputation of "snake oil" due to the business practices of the vast majority of firms in America.

Let me give you an anecdote to illustrate the size of the problem. A promising graduate of a fine university, "Navy" had four years of service as an officer in the Nuclear Navy and an additional four years of work in Nuclear Waste Disposal before being recruited by Owen. Navy was a buttoned-up, serious guy. The base pay he was offered was right in line with his classmates, but he was promised a bonus of 30% or more if:

1. The firm achieved its goals (which were carefully established to be reasonable).
2. He did his part as measured by the bonus system.

Eighteen months later, after his first full year at Owen Enterprises, the company had exceeded its goals, as everyone in the firm could plainly see, and Navy had had a fine year. When Owen presented him with a check equal to 35% of his base pay, Navy first turned pale then memorably said (his words not mine):

"You're shitting me?!"

To which Owen responded, "What did you expect?"

"I don't know, but this is unbelievable – I thought maybe I'd get (named a number that was about 5% of his base)."

Owen then understood what had happened. No one believed him when he told the truth about the bonus they would get because, as Navy later said (remember Navy is a salty sailor), "Everyone blows smoke up your ass about bonus."

Apparently this was true about everyone but Owen.

The most enjoyable task every year for Owen is delivering the first full-year bonus to staff at all levels. No one ever actually fainted, but there have been a few close calls. Propeller Head, a former pilot who did advanced statistical analysis, passed Owen in the hall with his larger-than-expected bonus. He was on his way to a jewelry store to purchase a lavish gift for his lovely wife and cleverly remarked, "Apparently top management has lost their minds." His bonus was pretty much exactly what the offer letter promised.

It's very sad really. Firms all over the country offer an incentive compensation plan that sounds great, but the moola never really materializes. The stories Owen has heard from disgruntled victims go on and on. Here are two that are representative.

A former member of senior management at a packaged goods firm and a current superstar salesperson for us, said the annual meeting at his prior employer (a Fortune top 50 firm) included division executives who would present business plans everyone in their group knew for a fact were fantasy. Then the CEO would tell everyone that they were the best team in the industry and he personally challenged them to "stretch" their goals by a further 15%. This became the firm goal that would be the basis for the bonus paid at the end of the year. Then the meeting was adjourned and every single person in the room knew there would be no bonus again that year!

Jayhawk (a Kansas graduate), a long-time loyal employee of another national firm, finally decided, in disgust, to leave and requested an interview with Owen Enterprises. Jayhawk explained, "My group doubled our profits, but no bonus was paid because the overall corporation failed to meet their goals."

Everyone should realize that when you offer a bonus to an individual you are trying to hire, they simply assume you are lying, and with good reason.

# 24 THE ACCOUNTING STATEMENTS

Managing the finances of Owen Enterprises in the early days was dead simple. In nine months, five projects were awarded and completed. Four people were hired. The firm operated out of an executive office facility which had receptionists, clerical staff, copiers, faxes, conference rooms and offices that were available on demand. Finance was pretty simple stuff really. Employee #2 wrote and signed the checks and watched the bank balance carefully, while Owen managed the Klients so he knew how we were doing.

As the firm grew, we leased office space and added sales staff, support staff, copiers, phone systems, and best of all, lots of Klients and projects which utilized a bewildering array of "sub-contractors" (275 last year!). The ability to answer, every single day, a simple and important question, "How are we doing?" can become almost impossible. You'd think you could get this number from the Accounting/Finance system on demand, at any time. Wrong, incredibly wrong!

The greatest and most reliable Controller Owen has ever known, "Kentucky" (complete with cute country accent) compiles "statements" faster than Owen has ever seen it done in the industry. It is pretty typical for businesses to get their accounting statements for March by sometime in mid-May. The statement represents how Owen Enterprises was doing as of six weeks ago. Imagine going to your doctor and when you ask "How am I doing?" the doctor responds, "Six weeks ago you were fine!" To Owen this was way too out of date. Our business and most businesses are dynamic.

Stuff happens every day. He wanted to know how we were doing right now.

In 2011 Owen Enterprises completed 750 projects for Klients. By the end of October, only 400 of them were completely finished so exact results were known for 53% of the sales we had made. A further 150 were awaiting invoices from subcontractors (many of whom seem to treat the sending of invoices like kids treat cleaning their rooms – very odd behavior). Two hundred projects, representing about 27% of the total sales to date, were "in process." The accounting department had virtually no data on them in the system yet.

When Owen wants to know how we are doing, he wants the data on how we are doing <u>now</u>. Considering everything we have in hand, what will the likely revenue and job costs be when it is all done? The Accounting Department cannot answer this and should not be expected to. Accounting exists as an important quality control check. Dot the i's and cross the t's is a favorite game and so is adding and subtracting and "balancing debits and credits."

An Italian, Luca Pacioli, is credited with inventing Double Entry Bookkeeping in the fifteenth century. It is regarded as some miraculous advance in Western Civilization. This comes as a real surprise to all the business majors who are required to study it in college and regard that particular course as cruel and unusual punishment! Double Entry Bookkeeping, according to accountants, is to business as Monet is to art. Go figure. Take some accounting statements to Paris and ask 10,000 visitors at the Musee de l'Orangerie which they'd rather look at, accounting statements or Monet's manic paintings of Water Lilies.

The SEC requires audited statements from public companies and they lead directly to tax returns. With any luck, the statements and the oak tree it takes every year to produce them, will look so imposing the IRS will allow you pay the taxes you say you owe (a system that works much better in the United States than it does in Greece), with no further interference in your life.

But you can't run your business by relying on accounting statements. Too much can happen between the last statements and today – way, way, way too much.

Fortunately, Owen has a secret weapon in the war on "How are we doing right now?"

## 25 COMPUTER GUY

The fifth employee of Owen Enterprises was the computer guy, CG. Owen first hired CG years earlier when he ran an office for Billie Enterprises. This was shortly after Owen got his very first personal computer, a portable Compaq that weighed *only* thirty pounds. Owen was excited about using spreadsheets, word processing (his handwriting was illegible even to himself so finding a secretary who could guess what he wrote was always a challenge), and graphics programs. However, to do so in those days required IT skills in something called DOS. The DOS manuals seemed to have been written in Latin so Owen was basically screwed. It was like having a Ferrari parked in the driveway, but missing the keys.

CG was recommended by an acquaintance of Owen's. The lad was only nineteen and a freshman at a local college. He arrived for his job interview while Owen was on the phone with an unpleasant Klient, who was explaining why Owen was not going to be awarded an important project despite a brilliantly designed proposal and competitive price that Owen had sweated blood over. In the tiny three-person office with the door open, young CG heard Owen slam the phone down. There is no truth to the claim that he broke the phone. It was easily glued back together. This was followed by a notebook binder containing the losing proposal being hurled against the office door, falling open, and pages scattering all over the floor. The unforgettable and sainted office secretary, Martha, calmly and without comment, picked up the pages, cleared a path into Owen's office, and announced, "Owen can see you now."

The kid was unfazed by this and clearly brilliant. Owen hired him on the spot with one small hurdle to overcome. Owen did not have authorization from his boss at Billie Enterprises to hire anyone for the "computer guy" role. Unfazed, he proposed to pay CG out of petty cash at the then prevailing minimum wage. CG accepted on the spot. Bogus petty cash requests were then made by the sainted Martha, approved by Owen, and dutifully paid to CG every week.

Two months later, Owen went to the home office and demonstrated a cost estimating program "he had been working on" to his Boss. The use of the program (ACE – Automated Cost Estimating) ultimately saved thousands of hours of manual work per year for Billie Enterprises – a huge home run. The Boss, memorably said:

"If I'd known you'd be this proficient with a computer, I'd have gotten you one much sooner."

"Um, actually Boss, the thing is, uh, there is one tiny detail I probably should have mentioned some time ago..." a squirming Owen began to explain.

Upon his return to the sales office, Owen was able to immediately double CG's salary and put him on the actual payroll. Owen and CG collaborated on a lot of work which saved time and money, and sped up office management processes. Collaboration is a cute word that suggests they both worked on the tasks, when in actuality, Owen stated very imposing goals and CG did all the work while Owen got much of the credit.

Three years later, CG was hire #5 at Owen Enterprises, over the quite sensible objections of employees #2, #3 and #4, who all loudly asserted, "We don't need an IT guy." All subsequently saw the error of their ways, but none admitted this to Owen.

Some of this story may seem archaic because computer networks are now accepted as an essential part of life ("... and then I realized if I carved out the middle of the stone I'd have a much lighter, round object that would still roll"), but it is still worth telling.

Over the next twenty-five years, Owen Enterprises was, and still is, the most efficient firm in the industry. The most correct title for Computer Guy is Efficiency Guy. The processes and programs put in place leveraged every single staff member. Our IT Department is like an incredible lubricant and Computer Guy created processes that allowed us to move at light speed. Beyond that, he personally trained, in one-on-one sessions, every single staff member for the next ten years. By then, he had a department of like-minded individuals who were the internal fire department. They were on call 24/7 and in your office within minutes to troubleshoot or retrain. Today, in every company we do business with, the promised response time for their systems help desk ranges from 24 hours to never. Owen cannot understand this at all.

CG was Owen's secret weapon to solve, in real time, the tricky "How are we doing?" problem. Weirdly, every time Owen talked to CG about a problem like this, CG would suggest a "Relational Database" as the solution. Owen decided he never had to understand this tool. He decided it was like "Double Entry Bookkeeping" – an abstract, complex, and strange concept that is best left to the Experts ("Geeks" is what he thought, but that is not politically correct, so he merely thought it).

CG created a system maintained by all of the Project Managers. Each Project Manager handles between three and eight unique projects at any one time (think of a home builder building all custom homes for example), and each project has seventy-five to one hundred cost categories (shipping, supplies, data collection, etc.). Costs change every week as unforeseen issues crop up or some savings are realized. Every week, Project Managers, who love this kind of detail work in their lives, update all project costs based on their best guesses for the costs in all categories. This information rolls up to the Weekly Report that shows revenue from all projects which had been started in the year, along with the estimated, real time, total job costs. The system CG built gives great insight into how we are doing right now.

CG had no sooner completed this stunning task when Owen engaged in a little "mission creep." This is where Owen spent two minutes praising the completion of the impossible task and then with great intensity said, "What I really needed though is a system that will tell me what the P&L will look like at the end of the year."

Unfazed, CG built another "Relational Database" which all the salespeople still use every week. They guess what the sales for each of their accounts will be at the end of the year. (The hopeful guess high, the pessimists guess low, but since magically there is an equal number of each, the overall total is pretty accurate.) This gives Owen a forecast for the year based on the most reliable information the twenty-five people, who are handling over one hundred Klients, possess at any point in time.

Year after year the guesses for the year-end sales have come within 3% of the actual figure. Owen came to trust this Management Information System implicitly. Hiring plans and capital expenditures are very precisely matched to the outlook for the year. This information ensures that the profit (me) is protected and grows year after year.

Profit is the grade a firm gets. It is the measure of how efficiently the capitalist is deploying and utilizing capital and labor. The Demons understandably were very annoyed at the development of these databases. Owen knows that when the Demons are annoyed, we are winning.

# 26 OWNERSHIP

Early on, Owen realized that anyone he hired was taking a huge risk and they would clearly be "worse off in the short run." No sane person would do that. Owen thought having sane people surrounding him was a good idea, so he had to craft an enticement (that word again) which would attract good people who were willing to take a risk. Short term loss for long term gain was the only move available on the board. So Owen offered stock.

Employee #2 joined for 15% of the stock, his salary was "accrued" (talk about risk), and the bonus plan was not in place. It turned out to be a real sweet deal, but it started out with lots of risk.

Employee #3 was paid at her then current rate and earned 1% of the outstanding stock each year for five years.

Both of these fantastic people are in Owen's all-time Hall of Fame of appreciated individuals. Both made bets that ultimately paid off handsomely by putting their careers on the line.

Many small firms start this way and then as they gain Klients, revenue and the trappings of success, can find and hire good people who do not <u>have</u> to be offered stock to entice them to join the firm. So the founders stop offering stock and keep all of the profits for themselves.

Owen, however, had a different plan.

One of the first books on starting your own business he read suggested that founders should have a plan in mind about whom they will sell their firm to from day one. This is sort of like stressing from the date of conception about where your children should go college. But the book (as books often are) was right.

Owen, who was in his forties, knew that someday (like today) he'd be sixty-five, and by then he would have a buyer for his business. He knew from Day One whom the buyer would be: the key employees.

Why? It was simple. If offering to let employees buy stock in a start-up business that was pretty much worthless could entice #2 and #3 to leave good jobs to join Owen Enterprises, then a stake in a profitable growing business would be very attractive to the kind of top notch talent he hoped to attract in the future. In economics this would be called a "Competitive Advantage."

Owen reasoned if he could attract and retain the best people, his firm would grow in value and even though his percentage of ownership would fall every year, the value of the stock he did hold onto would go up. I know this idea sounds like a shell game but it's not, it's just simple math. Think about it:

1. Sell 5% of the stock,
2. To an outstanding salesperson,
3. Who attracts profitable business to the firm,
4. Which drives the value of the firm up by anything more than 5%, and
5. Owen makes out like a bandit!

Everyone thought Owen was being nice because the buyers of the stock all made out quite well. However, the buyers themselves drove the value of the company up and Owen's stock was worth more than it would have been if he didn't sell any stock.

AND, (drum roll) he knew from day one whom he would sell the business to, which the book said was an important thing to figure out!

There is a last and terribly important reason to offer stock to people who can create growth; it is the fair thing to do.

Owen did not think he was being nice or generous – he honestly understood that he was being (here it comes again) greedy. Owen thought Greed could not only be good, but it could be perfect in this case.

Consider for a moment #19. She joined the firm in 1992. Since that date, she has accounted for over 15% of the firm's sales, which is a startling performance. She leads a large team of staff members who have learned a great deal from her. The work they produce is praised by Klients and the profits are solid. She is well compensated and her bonus, year in and year out, ranks first or second in the firm. Her personal efforts have raised the value of the firm. She is not just an employee, she is Capital. Her rewards should include:

- Base salary to compensate her for the hours she puts in.
- Bonus salary every year to compensate her for the results she achieved that year.
- Dividends – her share of the profits the firm earned that year.
- Capital Appreciation – to compensate her for her ability to drive the value of the firm.

Offering ownership on favorable terms to #19 and those like her is hardly a kind or generous gesture, it is simply fair compensation for her contributions.

# 27 THE DEAL

When the firm was not worth very much the ownership deal was simple. New employees either purchased stock or accepted stock as part of their compensation package. After that the next few purchasers were required to work for approximately eighteen months before being offered stock, but the price stayed pretty low and they were able to purchase stock for cash. The number of shares offered to the employee went down as the price went up.

For the last fifteen years, however, as the firm grew and prospered, the value of the firm and the stock shot up geometrically (that is how it works). It soon became necessary for purchasers to have access to financing in order for them to afford the shares. The firm got its bank to loan the money to prospective owners so they could buy stock. The offer to prospective owners was pretty simple:

1. They put up 25% of the purchase price.
2. Our bank lends them the rest.
3. We co-sign the note.
4. The purchaser pays for the stock using dividends they would not have received had they not bought the stock.

It is a sweet deal for the purchaser and a sweet deal for Owen who knows full well that even his very persuasive sales skills would not have attracted #19 and her peers into the firm, unless it was a better deal for them than the much safer alternative – stay safe and comfy right where they were.

Once an employee becomes an owner in a successful, growing firm, their commitment to the firm and effort level changes. Anyone who reads this could not doubt it for a minute. Owen was selling stock and buying growth and commitment to the firm.

But Owen remembered that the exit of the TRAITORS from Billie Enterprises had been very damaging. Good people (including Owen) who were Capital used the elevator to escape from Billie. They went down the street and their Klients went with them. The Klients they "took" with them apparently valued their services more than they valued the firm for which the TRAITORS worked. The value of Billie Enterprises went down. Beyond that, the TRAITORS soon attracted other staff members from Billie Enterprises, which further damaged the company's worth.

When Owen thought about this, he realized he needed to protect his firm in the event of a messy divorce like that. The Buy/Sell agreement every owner signs does just that. An owner of Owen Enterprises who leaves to go into competition must surrender their stock. In addition, in the case of a departure deemed to be particularly damaging to Owen Enterprises, certain penalties may be imposed:

- The stock can be reduced in value by 25%.
- The money can be paid out over four years.
- The owner may lose any dividends that might be paid.

In twenty-five years only one owner has suffered these penalties. Many others have become disgruntled at times, but the terms above tempered their responses to all situations that made them unhappy.

# 28 SUCCESSION PLANNING

In all fields of professional practice, the retirement of a senior sales person or partner sends spasms of fear throughout the firm. The Klient, who has come to be utterly dependent upon the retiring partner, may look around and then place their work with a competitive firm. This was an area where the Demons were especially active because no one Owen knew seemed immune to this issue. However, applying the learning from the Elevator Problem, Owen listed all the issues and then tried to imagine how to address them one by one.

In most firms in America, if #2 is going to retire, he would mention this in passing a couple of months in advance (or less) to give the employer time to buy the obligatory watch and plan a modest "Farewell #2" lunch. #2 would then collect his last paycheck and bid the firm goodbye. The firm would hastily send the new team to meet with his Klients, hoping they can somehow hang onto the business, but knowing they should be planning on losing at least 65% of it very quickly.

Owen spent time thinking about why this scenario was true and tried to think of some way to entice (that word again) #2 to:

1. Announce his intent to retire well in advance (two years).
2. Identify a logical successor from among the current staff.
3. Spend two years training and developing the successor.
4. Put the successor into an increasingly visible role.
5. Share sales credit with the successor.

6. Back out of the account gradually so no one noticed he was gone and no one had a substantially negative reaction to his exit.

What enticement do you think Owen decided to use to have #2 follow these "Good Owner Exit Guidelines?"

A. Promises of undying gratitude
B. #2's own sense of obligation to the firm
C. Threats
D. Money

If you said D, you'd be right – Money the undefeated, all-time, world champion enticement.

Under the "Good Owner Exit Guidelines," the retiring shareholder is permitted to hold some stock for two years after retirement. This is a substantial inducement – all profits are paid out in the form of dividends to shareholders every year. In addition, since Owen Enterprises was growing and profitable the value of shares typically grew every year. The "retiree" had plenty of incentives to do that right thing and they all did.

# 29  MANAGEMENT EVOLUTION

In the early days, Owen Enterprises had very experienced staff who had worked together in the past and they all fell into step (motivated no doubt by the ever-present Demons). They simply did their jobs right. With a staff of four to eight experienced people, almost no management is necessary. A state of nearly continuous crisis prevailed (brought on by no small amount of over-promising to Klients by Owen), and everyone did a little of everything. At the end of the year the bonus was handed out, celebrated and then they returned to start over in the New Year.

## Use of memos evolves

The firm grew to a point where fifteen people attended the Monday Morning Meeting, our sole management tool in those days. One day Owen "invented" a management tool (re-invented is a better word). July 4th fell on a Thursday and he felt a four-day weekend would be nice for everyone. With only ten employees present that morning, he was afraid he might not get the message out to everyone using the two communication tools that heretofore had sufficed:

- Shouting down the hall - "Hey everyone! We were just awarded the big project Gary had us bid on!"
- Going from office to office to speak personally to all employees (very time consuming, especially since they were not all in the office when he arrived).

Owen thought about this for a moment and remembered the memo, a much hated system, which in prior life, was used by management mainly as disinformation. Here is a prime example:

| What was written | How to read the memo |
|---|---|
| To: All Highly Valued Staff<br>From: VP Bob R. Smyth<br>Re: Retirement of Henry | To: Peons<br>From: The Lying Asshole<br>Re: Firing of Henry |
| Henry, our much beloved, long time VP has decided to retire to spend more time with his family. | Henry, an expensive, trouble-making asshole who I hate, was fired today and beaten. |
| Best of luck, Henry. | Go suck an egg, Henry. |

Like bonus plans that promised the world but never actually delivered any cash to actual people, the typical memo has the credibility in the business world that the news media has in the Soviet Union.

Owen had never used a memo at Owen Enterprises because of all the terrible experiences he and others had previously suffered from past abuses. Early in his career Owen had bumped into the unfortunate aforementioned Henry and congratulated him on this career milestone. Henry then burst into tears and started shouting. This was an extremely unpleasant but memorable experience for Owen.

But just this once, perhaps sending a memo might ensure that all staff members got the good news to take Friday, July 5th off from work. They did and were grateful.

Soon memos became a useful tool at Owen Enterprises and they always told the truth. As parents from time immemorial have told their children, telling the truth all the time will earn trust. Getting a reputation for lying corrodes any relationship and if management needs anything from the staff, it is trust.

## Committees evolve naturally

Soon after adopting the use of memos, other issues began to pop up that seemed to tie up a lot of time at the Monday Morning Meeting. With fifteen people in the room, any individual issue was of extreme interest to five, of minor interest to five more, and of no interest whatsoever to the remaining five. All were painfully aware that no Klient work was actually done in the meeting and getting out of the room left them free to do work that earned money.

One morning a really funny thing happened. The healthcare plan discussion was putting the no-interest group to sleep. One brave soul said, "Whatever you want to do here is fine with me; I have work to do," and left. Instantly, the other four members of the no-interest group left with the same lame excuse to do work that earned money.

The minor-interest crowd quickly woke up and realized that by switching to the no-interest team, they could also go do their work and earn money. Without a word they got up, left the meeting, and went to work.

The remaining extremely-interested team lost two members who suddenly realized they might fall behind in the bonus pool. This left three people who strangely seemed to care more about the company healthcare plan than they did about money. They renamed themselves:

**The Committee of concerned staff members who care about the health care plan which all of the company desperately needs while the rest of you greedy bastards don't care about anything but your own bonus. So, we will do our best to get a plan that benefits everyone even if it personally costs us a few bucks of bonus money.**

The remaining committee members did, indeed, tackle their tasks with a renewed sense of urgency, and we saw that small, highly motivated committees could effectively craft "acceptable" solutions to common problems quite quickly. Then they, too, could go back to doing work the Klients wanted, which created profit for the firm and bonus for them. It turns out that committee meetings do not need to include everyone, and highly motivated committee members will soon find ways to compromise on their differences, lest they spend so much time trying for perfection that they get no bonus at all

Soon other committees naturally evolved to address a myriad other issues and the firm was well served by the natural goodness of staff members who had real interest, expertise and a long-term perspective on important topics.

Owen added a category to the bonus plan called Management and money was steered to individuals who spent time on these critically important tasks. These points were not published each week so as not to distract anyone from the shorter term, more critical goals of solving Klient problems.

## Managers naturally evolve

Soon Owen Enterprises had twenty-five employees including four Klient Service Team Leaders (Owen insisted on calling them Peddlers internally, but they preferred the more elegant title) and seven Project Managers. The Project Managers shared a common responsibility in the firm, but worked on different teams. The teams were Klient based and the Project Managers reported to and got work assignments from the Team Leaders. If someone wanted to take the day off, got sick, was traveling on an assignment, or had vacation scheduled, they had to get somebody else to cover for them.

#3, the most senior Project Manager, had previously been a manager at Billie Enterprises and several of the other Project Managers had "reported" to her. Although this formal reporting structure was not in place at Owen Enterprises, over time Owen noticed the Project Managers occasionally lunching together, after which scheduling issues magically disappeared. There were rumors that the lunches also served as group therapy sessions, in which stories of Owen's unrealistic promises could be aired out. Since this venting appeared to be therapeutic, Owen began paying for the lunches, and "raised the ante with respect to overpromising!" Somehow it all seemed to work out.

Thus, #3 became the ombudsperson for the Project Management Team. She dealt with vacations, sick days, maternity leave, and so forth. Inevitably, she became a veritable fount of valuable advice to less experienced team members. She began to schedule meetings where others presented best practices or sometimes they spent the whole hour venting. In any case, this process serves us well even today. #3 and other ombudspersons get credit (money) in the bonus pool, but as with committee work, it is secondary to Klient work...

Note that the Project Managers continue to report to the Team Leaders. Their evaluations are done by the Team Leaders, who also award promotions, raises, and participate in bonus fine-tuning. The Team Leaders are responsible to the Klients, so the reporting structure and rewards system is based entirely on keeping the oxygen flowing.

## Bonus as a management system

It became very plain to see that the rewards system was driving behavior. The professors who wrote about "clear line of sight to the bottom line" were on to something. Owen would rename this "clear proportional access to the money created by productive behavior." When the staff stands to personally benefit in a meaningful way from doing Klient work well, it becomes kind of difficult to get them to do anything else.

For example, for years many employees refused to take all the vacation they were entitled to. They offered three explanations:

1. We were busy and I didn't want to let the team/Klients down.
2. I can use the bonus money.
3. You pay me for the unused vacation time and I can use the money.

All three have merit and standing. Owen worried about this feature of the rewards-based culture he had built and wished more people would take all of their vacation to rest and spend time with their families. The staff seemed to have a totally different mindset, and the Klients loved the fact that "their team" was almost always available to them.

After years of trying moral suasion to get the staff to see he was right, to no effect whatsoever, Owen modified company policy to limit the number of unused days that would be paid for at the end of the year. Like magic, the amount of unused vacation decreased to that for which he was willing to pay. It seems that reason number one, not wanting to let the team and Klient down, played only a small role in deciding to work instead of taking time off.

The staff knows what they want in this arena and Owen finally decided to stop trying to manage their personal lives and stick to managing the firm.

## The Chief

By 2001 the firm was a 14-year old teenager and, like teenagers everywhere, it was a challenge to manage. The mostly informal processes that   served us well when we were small and comprised mainly of experienced professionals were not generally effective in the infinitely more complex firm we had become. Issues such as the following came up on a regular basis.

1. I don't like my team.
2. "He's touching me" (age-old back seat complaint of all siblings).
3. I haven't been promoted in five years.
4. I need to vent and don't know where to go.
5. Is there any way to get training/education paid for?
6. Et cetera
7. Et cetera

Owen, who mainly (completely?) focused on Klients and growth, found himself completely out of his depth on this and many other issues. Somehow though he was lucky – he always seemed lucky. Napoleon, when asked what quality he most valued in his generals, replied without hesitation, "The best ones are lucky."

Owen's luck held when the soon-to-be COO (The Chief) contacted him to say he was finished living in Disney World (literally) and wanted to return to the land of his birth, which was cursed with five months of grey, wet winters.

The Chief had loads of management experience, seemed like a fine addition to the team, and, shrewdly, had even less hair than Owen despite being much younger. This created an instant chemistry between the two.

The Chief was presented with sixty-two staff members in six different departments and instructed to "take care of that stuff." A couple of years later at an industry conference, The Chief, when asked what his responsibilities were, said, "I do everything Owen doesn't want to do." The laughter in the room was earsplitting. Owen, while hurt, had to admit he had learned to take all knotty management issues to the Chief with the request he "take care of this" as he bolted for the door to catch another flight to see a Klient or prospective Klient.

A peer once asked Owen, now that he was a successful CEO of a growing firm, why he still traveled 100-120 days per year and Owen replied, "When I'm on the road all I have is opportunities. When I'm in the office all I have is problems."

This perfectly captures why The Chief was so desperately needed. Owen was very good with Klients and had cultivated a wide circle of acquaintances on the Klient side that he tirelessly pursued. (The expense account bills for dinners with fine French wines seemed a little over the top, but the results spoke for themselves.) He lacked patience, which is a virtue in a salesperson but a fatal weakness in management.

Owen knew what he was good at and recognized that The Chief, a man of seemingly infinite patience with a talent for really listening, had the complementary skills Owen Enterprises needed to get from teenager to young, mature professional.

Over the years The Chief planned, organized, motivated, and controlled the staff. He earned a reputation for fairness and even-handed treatment of everyone. He became a whiz at finance.

Once a banker asked, "Do you have any rough idea of your average bank balance over the last couple of years?"

The Chief instantly tapped his computer screen and showed the very impressed banker the end-of-week cash balance for every week over the last twenty years. He also built a masterful sheet that did a fine job of forecasting the ending monthly cash balance for the next twelve months.

As we grew from 62 employees to 140, The Chief soon needed help. A number of people on the staff were groomed to be important parts of our management structure.

One of these was #8, a fabulous and ambitious twenty-something young woman who applied for the receptionist/printing/shipping/everything-we- could-think-of job, despite the fact that she had a position with the local Major League Baseball club and was the envy of everyone who knew her. When Owen asked why she would leave such a prestigious position to work for a tiny, unknown firm she said, "They are not professional in their office operations and I want more from my job than just the chance to hang around with wealthy, arrogant baseball players." Owen hired her on the spot. Long story short – she is now the VP of Human Resources, a partner in the firm, and the most respected person in the building.

Another important part of our management structure is #65, the Kentucky-born Controller, whom I spoke about earlier. Perfection comes easily to her and her team, and that is very reassuring to everyone when it comes to handling the money. She is invariably kind and thoughtful but all are advised to toe the line or she can fire up the Demons and see to it that you do. She has built a small but extremely efficient team that gets the job done.

## The evolution thing

In large businesses, many practices that once made sense, such as memos, committees and management practices evolve into bizarre, ineffective and even counterproductive tools. One large firm in Owen's industry had several hundred (!) committees. Everyone knew they had too many, and none of them seemed to be really effective. They decided that the way to tackle the problem (I kid you not) was to create a Committee to Reduce the Number of Committees.

Starting from scratch, with no management system, is pretty interesting. Owen learned that the traditional tools do become useful at a certain point in time and only then should they be used. (Think about sending a memo to the only other staff member, whom you have lunch with every day.)

At every step along the way from a one-person firm to four, then twelve, then 25, then 62, then 90, and now 140, we built our management system to fit the staff we had and then went to work applying The Formula. Because The Formula worked, we regularly added staff and facilities, and created a more complex firm that needed additional management. It would be nice to report that these needs were always anticipated, but that would be fiction.

The truth is the system that worked well with four people broke down when there were twelve people. Stress was created and then a new system was devised. We constantly outran our management capabilities and then had to scramble to fix the problems. Some contend it would have been a far better idea to have anticipated the impact of the growing staff on our needs. On the other hand, allowing management solutions to evolve in response to breakdowns insured we never had more management than we needed.

Beyond this, Owen resisted writing policies to cover hypothetical problems at every turn. He reasoned, correctly, as it turns out, that the context of the situation that really occurs will drive the solution the first time you encounter it. Then you have a precedent you can go back to for guidance when the same situation comes up in the future.

# 30 BLACK SWANS

In his book, *The Black Swan: The Impact of the Highly Improbable*, Nassim Taleb introduced the idea of Black Swan events. These are highly improbable and unpredictable events that can swamp even the most careful plans. Some Black Swans, such as the Great Depression and World War II, are very damaging. Some, such as the Internet, create vast opportunities. Running a company and surviving or even thriving when Black Swan events occur without warning teaches very vivid lessons.

In the early years, attracting staff was extremely tricky. The best people, the ones you wanted and needed, were all gainfully employed by firms that valued and paid them and seemed like a safe place to work. Owen Enterprises had little history and only a handful of employees. It definitely didn't have an exercise facility or cafeteria. In fact, it seemed like a poorly equipped island. Joining Owen Enterprises was a very risky proposition for a talented player.

Owen found that he had to use all of his considerable sales skills to attract employees. He was extremely grateful to every one of them and felt an obligation to them. As the business grew, paid terrific bonuses, and recorded growing profits every year, Owen Enterprises' success became his best sales pitch. It seemed easy and almost automatic, and we were lulled into thinking it was always going to be easy.

Early in 2001, the forecast suggested that the year would be a fine one, just like all the prior years, with a 15% growth forecasted. By late August we were 12% ahead of the previous year. Everything seemed on track. Owen hired based on forecasts so when new Klients or assignments were forthcoming, we would have the staff we needed and the work would be performed perfectly.

The national trauma we experienced on 9/11 left us all in shocked disbelief. The tragedy was a shared human experience on a massive scale. Understandably the entire economy stalled, work dried up, and Owen Enterprises experienced its first year with a decline in revenue, 5% from 2010. This meant Owen Enterprises was about 20% overstaffed. By early January the outlook for 2002 was also bleak.

Owen was paralyzed. Laying off people whom he'd worked so hard to hire was simply unacceptable to him. He favored People over Profits and held onto the staff. Had this been made public, he would have gotten awards:

## Local Businessman Retains Staff In Spite Of Sales Declines

He boldly decided to eliminate raises for the entire staff and created his own "wishing and hoping" plan that fantasized a highly unlikely increase in revenue in 2002. This was not going to happen. It would be sort of like the home team hitting two grand slams in the ninth inning to win the game 8-7. The top line was pretty much flat, below the prior best year, and everyone felt it. Morale sagged, Profits declined, and we experienced three years of pain with too much staff and overhead.

Some of the employees had fine years during that time but they did not get the rewards they deserved for a very simple reason:

Owen was not doing his job. He knows this in retrospect and he learned a very harsh lesson from the experience. Some very good people left seeking "greener pastures." As it turns out, your very best people will cruelly care more about their own welfare and their families than they do about the firm.

Free snacks, private offices, fun parties, and respect for staff mean almost nothing if the boss does not do his job – no matter how painful. The staff began to lose respect for Owen. They knew he needed to "Man Up" and right-size the company, but he didn't do it.

Fortunately, another Black Swan event occurred in 2004. A directly competitive firm in our hometown disintegrated and a number of very fine sales executives, desperate for jobs and looking for a friendly port in a storm, joined our firm. We were off to the races again! It's comparable to turnovers in football games; we'd caught a break and took advantage of it. Owen Enterprises experienced a phenomenal growth spurt, the bonus pool was overflowing and we were hot again.

In 2008, the Black Swan hit again in the fourth quarter – the economy imploded and business dried up. In August, we had been running 20% ahead of the prior year but we finished the year 5% behind. It was déjà vu all over again. But this time Owen was more disciplined because of the experiences he'd lived through in 2001. He had grown up, accepted the responsibilities of leadership, and so he did the right thing, painful as it was.

We had to right-size the firm. In January of 2009, we fired three very nice but unproductive employees whom we had kept around in order to dodge the unpleasantness of firing them. This is a disease that is all too common in business and does no one any good. Then, we laid off twelve good people who were frankly not quite as good/talented/hard working/reliable as the rest of the staff and cut spending on overhead items by 25%.

Owen did not enjoy this but now looks back on it as a maturing experience. In 2001, in his eagerness to protect his staff, he punished the best among them with poor performance and a lousy bonus and created fear that the good times were over. We unintentionally downsized as some of our best people made the logical decision to move on. In 2008, Owen right-sized the firm, and fifteen perfectly nice, but not our best, people lost their jobs.

Many of the overhead items we cut in 2008 were missed by the remaining staff but they came to terms with the changes. At the end of the year the pain of the decline in top line revenue was more than offset by the 25% reduction in labor and overhead. Profits were up! Bonus was up! Morale was great and we returned to growth by 2010.

This tale of two challenges in 2001 and 2008 has an important moral:

**An Owner who favors people over profits
hurts his most capable people.**

**An Owner who favors profits over people
protects his most capable people.**

As heartless as this may seem to some readers, the lesson cannot be escaped. It is worth realizing that the marginal players on every team know it. The other players, the stars, know who the marginal players are. The staff members who lost their jobs in 2008 were not marginal human beings – their skill set and personalities just did not fit perfectly into our environment. Most of them went on to find positions that fit them better. I believe they are happier today in the jobs they found than they would have been if we had "let" them continue to work at Owen Enterprises.

The downsizing that took place after the 2001 event cost Owen some of his "A" players. The team by the end of the year was, on average, not as talented as it had been before. In 2008, by downsizing the least productive staff members, he increased the average talent level in the organization and clearly alerted the entire team that we were in a tough situation.

The impact on the remaining staff after the layoffs was complex. Initially they were, of course, fearful and concerned for their friends who had been "made redundant." They were also grateful to still be working at Owen Enterprises and got a dramatic wake-up call about the situation. They all redoubled their efforts and created a fine year and a platform on which we could grow. Owen came to believe that when he shouldered his responsibilities and did his job, his best people had less reason to take the elevator down at night, walk out the door, and keep right on going to another job.

Management cannot afford sentimentality. It must ruthlessly protect the firm. Robert E. Lee once famously remarked while watching the drama at Gettysburg unfold in front of him, "To be a good soldier you must love the army. To be a good commander you must be able to order the death of the thing you love." Fortunately in business we don't have mortal responsibilities, but to be a great business leader your first and foremost responsibility must be to protect the firm. You cannot do that by refusing to right-size the staff in the face of challenging times – you only weaken the firm and put it into a life- threatening condition.

# 31 OWEN ARRIVES

Peter Profit noticed a stirring in the back of the room as Owen arrived. Peter motioned him to the stage, introduced him and, after a quick comment to let Owen know where he was in the talk, sat down. Owen approached the lectern and then addressed the group.

"I'm sure Peter has done a fine job of telling our story. I'd like to add some personal remarks in several areas."

# 32  FEAR

Shortly after I left my very good job with a firm I still respect and love, an odd thing began to happen. Lots of people would say, "I'm going to do that someday, leave good old Balago Industries where I hate working, and do something on my own." Some of these people would seek me out to brainstorm plans and ideas. No one ever actually left. The first step is almost impossible, especially if you have been successful (e.g. making more money than Dad did or more than you ever really thought you'd make).

In the years before I quit, I created business plans over and over again, but could not find the nerve to do anything. On at least three occasions I threw them away and resolved to become a new, improved Owen, rejoin the team, and stop driving my management crazy. It never lasted for long. Fear and greed were locked in mortal combat and fear was winning. Fear almost always wins. People hate to fail so we don't take as much risk as we should.

I was as afraid to try this as I have ever been. I spent a year in Vietnam as an electronics technician. I had no experiences like those in the movie *Platoon*, but I did have some pretty real moments. I was based at Cu Chi. This was the base camp outside of Saigon that famously had the 25th infantry division above ground and a North Vietnamese regiment in tunnels under the base camp! My regular barber, a sweet guy, turned out to be cutting hair by day and shooting mortars at us by night.

The night the Tet Offensive started in 1968, I was on guard duty on the perimeter. I heard rockets flying over the bunker I was manning. They sounded like freight trains and then exploded with an unforgettable sound and concussion. They blew stuff up all over the place.

That night I was young, stoned, and stupid. Years later the thought of leaving a secure job when I had a wife, a child and responsibilities was at least that frightening. That was when I met The Demons.

One night I was so upset at my old firm that I painted over the sign in front of the building as a protest. Everyone assumed it was me, but I have never admitted it until now. I was still too scared to quit my job. I kept talking about it and thinking about it but I couldn't find the nerve. A good-ol'-boy accountant buddy of mine once told me, "This is an itch you are going to have to scratch someday," and I guess he was right. The day I resigned and walked out of the old building was surreal. I felt like I was walking on quicksand. I was terrified.

It turns out that inside all of us is the Tom Hanks character who was marooned on an island in *Castaway*. After crying and shouting at the sea, he decided to live. He built a structure, found food and water, made use of the stuff around him and then began to work on a way out of the mess he was in.

Oddly, the fear was worse <u>before</u> I quit. Once you are committed to something like this, a feeling of peace comes over you

— I guess it's sort of like the *Butch Cassidy and the Sundance Kid* scene on the cliff.

Butch says, "I can't swim."

The Kid replies, "The fall will probably kill you."

Take the plunge into a very threatening situation and your mind expunges all extraneous thoughts. You don't have time to be scared. You have to be fully committed to the thing you are doing and channel your fear into determination.

The Demons do the best they can to shake your confidence but they really only come out at night. By daybreak your drive to succeed will take over. I regard the first two years of Owen Enterprises as the most productive time in my life.

# 33 WHO WILL BUY THE FIRM FROM ME?

I was shocked when one of the books I read early on said I should know right away who I would sell the firm to. During those early days, being worth anything seemed preposterous, and we might have sold out for a song at some of the low points. Try this idea. Go home from work and mention to your spouse, for whom you have not produced a paycheck in three months, two weeks, two days, and one hour, that you simply don't know who you will sell this business to in 25 years. It's the loony bin for you. Really – lots of drugs and a long night's sleep.

Oddly, however, it should be on the horizon almost right away. There are four common options to think about when considering what will become of your firm when you are no longer around.

### Ruin your children's lives.

Work your children into your business and leave it to them. Well, the IRS will have a thing or two to say about that. "Your kids now owe a billion dollars in taxes – and cash would be nice by the close of business today." Then there is the main question. Are your kids any good at this thing and how will the staff (25 years older and infinitely more experienced at this line of work) feel about that? I think that kid in Korea, Kim Jong Un, is scared to death and he should be. His direct reports don't look all that thrilled with the new 22-year-old "Esteemed Leader for Life." I never really thought about that option and I think my kids and my staff are all relieved.

**Destroy the thing you worked so hard to build and ruin the lives of your staff, Klients and suppliers.**

(Aka, cash in your chips by selling the firm to a big firm in your industry.) This happens all the time. The transactions in our industry are stupid. The big boys (who are like Darth Vader – wizards much smarter than you with very cool weapons) will "buy" firms for seven times earnings on a day when they are trading for fifteen times earnings, so they get a steal on day one. Think that through carefully. In addition, they will eliminate almost everything Peter Profit mentioned we do to build staff loyalty and effort, including tearing down the offices to install cubes. Seriously, one of them said that was imperative. This is so the other 10,000 employees in their firm aren't resentful of the new division and its cushy facilities.

Selling your firm, your life's work, to one of the Big Boys is kind of like signing up to be a member of the Mob. Actually, it's worse than the Mob because you and all your key people forego all profits for the next three years but you have to work for them, and then you can't compete with them for five more years. This is more one-sided than the U.S. Marines vs. Grenada.

**Go into partnership with the government and the bank.**

Employee Stock Ownership Plans (ESOP's) are interesting except for one small problem. You sell the firm to the entire staff, not just the senior resources who are able to drive success, and then get a bank to finance the transaction. The Federal Government "oversees" ESOP's. So you go into business with the government and a bank. The government sends over some retired TSA staff to order you around and the bank calls every day to ask, "How is it going?" Sadly, the government is lousy at governing and even worse at business. The bank will try to make sure you pay the loan off real, real, real, soon. This is a nightmare only the Demons would love.

**Live forever working hard all the time.**

Somehow this did not seem realistic, although at times it was the most attractive option.

We took none of those options. Today I'm 65 and I've already sold 65% of my firm to the most senior members of the team – the strategic assets. They bought stock years ago, participated in the profits we made, and continued to reinvest and drive the value of the firm. They are getting 65% of the profits from the firm and can use them to buy me out. That is financially very simple math. So I began to sell my firm almost from the beginning to senior, strategically critical staff. They bought stock at prices that seem like a real bargain now, plus they accumulated dividend income that puts them in a position to buy more stock today.

What I got from this is a committed, outstanding team of loyal employees who, through their efforts, drove the value of the firm. This seems to me to be a viable strategy for a professional services firm. It certainly worked for us.

In many cases, the senior staff have owned shares and participated in the running of the company for years. They understand the business strategy. They have been in training to run the firm for years. They've served on the Board and had to take part in making some tough decisions. They are, in a word, ready for the challenge and they deserve the rewards. I will become Chairman of the Board and plan to meddle in their decisions as little as possible. I want and need them to succeed. I hope my advice, based on 40 years of experience, will continue to be an asset.

Our owners, staff, Klients, and suppliers should anticipate no fundamental change in the way we do business with them. By contrast with every other "succession strategy," this is the least disruptive alternative.

The owners will have to select a leader and then they will be well served to support the one they choose. We have a carefully constructed ownership agreement that gives the person selected the power to run the company. The government is not involved in any of our decisions and we like it that way. We pay our taxes and they leave us alone. We owe the bank no money and aim to keep them out of our business as well.

# 34 SUCCESS MARKER IN THE FUTURE

Every business has a very long "to do" list every day. Under new leadership, decisions will be made about the priorities. Priorities break down into strategic imperatives and tactical plans. Imagine each one was a playing card in a deck. The strategic imperatives have to be identified first (that makes them Aces – the most powerful cards in the deck). Once they have been identified, the tactical goals and their priority become easy to sort out. For the last 25 years our strategic imperatives have been:

1. Ownership by the senior staff is the foundation of our ability to succeed in the long term.
2. The Klient is King and every decision should reinforce that idea to them and to us.
3. Profits are the byproduct of success and the source of new capital.
4. Growth is essential if we are to accomplish the first imperative. Apply The Formula over and over again to grow and manage the growth.

Every tactical alternative should be one that reinforces or increases the likelihood of success of the strategic plan. Any tactical alternative that undermines the essential strategic goals should be abandoned.

# 35  PROFITS ARE MAGIC

In a perfectly competitive marketplace every business has to price their services in a way that wins the work. There are two way of doing this – one very difficult and one that is pretty simple. The difficult way is to guess all the costs perfectly, then decide on a required margin above your costs. Your price to the Klient is your cost plus margin. This involves hiring brilliant accountants at a time when you have no substantial amounts of money to monitor. If you are successful you will need accountants at some point but no one needs them immediately.

The easy way to price work is to find out what your competitors are charging for this sort of work and offer to do the work for that price (or a little less!). One of the TRAITORS shared this wisdom with me more than 30 years ago and I am deeply indebted to him for this advice.

My fifteen years in the business prior to going out on my own had given me the ability to guess competitive prices pretty accurately. I figured if other firms could remain in business charging their prices, then so could we. Once we won some business, we tried to do the work so efficiently that we could cover all our costs and have something called **profits** left over. The most efficient firms win!

When we became profitable the impact was **magical.** Our confidence in our business model grew; we took more risks, chased larger accounts, hired more great people and won more business – which was profitable! Profits enabled us to pay great bonuses, invest in terrific facilities and offer fine benefits. Profits allowed us to be aggressive. The growth we could brag about to prospective Klients and new staff increased our odds of winning both business and staff. The whole thing feeds on itself and profits are the irreplaceable magic ingredient.

Oddly, to the general public, profit has somehow acquired a bad reputation – kind of like OJ Simpson – famous and popular years ago but now tawdry and shameful. Obscene is a word that is often attached to profits. This is very sad. The profit the pharmaceutical industry achieves from selling patented drugs is their fair return for the billions of dollars they spend researching drugs that never make it to market. The oil industry gets lots of criticism for "unfair profits" but the investments they make in technologies that never pan out or "drilling dry holes" has to be recovered somehow. If we begin to assault firms like this they will inevitably invest less, discover less, and future generations will all suffer the consequences.

To an entrepreneur, making a profit is like being at the top of the Mt. Everest. The view is worth the risk. The appearance of profits is akin to the proverbial rabbit in the hat – *magic* and wondrous. The absence of profits for Owen Enterprises would have meant that the Demons were right and I had no business starting a business.

Success at creating profits requires risk taking, careful budgeting, and lots of management of the resources in ways that maximize productivity. Profits are not a dirty word – they are a noble achievement.

## 36 PROFITS AND PEOPLE

There is a great hue and cry in the country about diabolical businesses that put profits before people – this is simply mysterious to all businessmen. Sometimes firms do put people before profits. I did this in 2001. At the time it seemed like the right thing to do. In retrospect I weakened my firm, prolonged the agony of the downturn and while I protected the jobs for the less productive members of the staff, I did them no real favors. Their more productive, talented, hard working co-workers knew some of their neighbors were not pulling their weight. The group that should have been laid off knew they were damaging the team. Bonus, profits and share prices sagged, which weakened our firm. We were headed toward failure. If the 2008 meltdown had taken place in 2004 it could have destroyed our weakened firm. It happens all the time. We got lucky that the next external event was favorable for us. Luck saved us that time.

In 2008, as challenging as it was, we identified fifteen staff members we simply had no real work for in view of a painful contraction in our business. These fine people got a generous settlement, had a difficult and fearful couple of months and then found jobs more perfectly suited to their skills, abilities and temperaments.

The remaining staff recognized that a correct, if painful, decision had been made by management to strengthen the team and protect our future. They saw management had done its job. They pulled together and produced a fine year despite a substantial loss of revenue. This set the stage for a return to growth and success and now we are better able to weather a downturn should one occur, because we are healthier. This health is very clearly indicated by our profit percentage and growth rate.

If you want to be the leader of a group of people, you have to be prepared to do the actual job, which has at least two sides to it. One part is pleasant and the other not so pleasant, but each are equally important.

Delivering a generous bonus, promoting fine people, celebrating successes, treating the staff with respect and dignity, and dealing with personal tragedies among the staff with consideration and tact will give anyone in my position a warm feeling of pride. The Demons go into a deep depression when you do these things.

Firing nice people who can't really perform the job, making layoffs when business reversals require it, reprimanding staff when they behave in an unacceptable manner and making hard decisions to abandon programs that are not creating opportunities (folding your hand with thousands in the pot and admitting failure) are all part of management as well. Every time you duck these responsibilities you lose credibility and trust.

Almost every leader does the first part well. Many leaders avoid or – and this really sucks – delegate the second part. The staff always knows when the leader is doing his job. You get points for doing both parts of the job well and thus gain credibility and trust from your team.

# 37  THE LONG RUN

The framework for decisions is always interesting. I enlisted in the Army for four years in 1966 just ahead of the draft. I signed up for four years instead of the two I would have served if drafted. Because I enlisted I got training in electronics and the GI bill paid for four years of college.

I was offered jobs right out of the military that would have paid a handsome salary for me to use my electronics training in industry. Some job options were pretty attractive but the lure of a college education proved overwhelming. I put off the temptation of a fine salary and benefits in favor of getting a college education in business that I thought might pay off in the long run.

When people ask me for career advice when they are facing several alternative job offers, I have always asked them:

1.  Where do you want to be in five years?
2.  Which job alternative gets you closer to that goal today?
3.  Take that job even if it pays less today!

Way too many people select the best short term alternative. Years later they end up somewhere, but seldom do they end up happy or really fulfilled. The decisions that will be best in the long term almost always require some kind of short term sacrifice. It just works that way.

This type of decision making is called "delaying gratification." There has been some fascinating research on this topic.

The **Stanford marshmallow experiment** was a study on deferred gratification conducted in 1972 by psychologist Walter Mischel of Stanford University. A marshmallow was offered to very young children. If the child could resist eating the marshmallow in front of them for 15 minutes, they were promised two marshmallows instead of one. The scientists analyzed how long each child resisted the temptation of eating the marshmallow, and whether or not resisting the temptation had an effect on their future success.

The findings of this test showed that the children (age 4!) who resisted eating the marshmallow in front of them so they might enjoy two marshmallows later:

- were more likely eight years later to be described by their parents as competent,
- had higher SAT scores 12 years later, and
- were more likely to complete college.

Life is a long run. Success in the long run is all that really matters. At every turn we are presented with alternatives and some of the short term "baubles" are pretty attractive. A person who goes through life with a laser-like focus on the long run and a decision process that favors the options that best enhance their achievement of long-term goals will, almost certainly, live a fuller, happier and more successful life.

I knew a long time ago I wanted to start a firm. I had some clear ideas on how to run one and I was determined from the beginning that I would sell it to the staff that helped me build it. At every turn I tried to think about the long-term consequences. It worked out better than I ever imagined and

## "we all lived happily ever after."